ART BOOKS

FROM CRESCENT MOON PUBLISHING

Leonardo da Vinci
by James Pearson

Early Netherlandish Painting
by Rosalind Mutter

Piero della Francesca
by Naomi Haskell

Giovanni Bellini
by Julia Davis

Eric Gill: Nuptials of God
by Anthony Hoyland

Minimal Art and Artists In the 1960s and After
by Laura Garrard

Postwar Art
by George Knighton

Vincent van Gogh: Visionary Landscapes
by Stuart Morris

Max Beckmann
by Stuart Morris

Egon Schiele: Sex and Death in Purple Stockings
by D. Simon Eade

Mark Rothko: The Art of Transcendence
by Julia Davis

Jasper Johns
by L.M. Poole

Brice Marden
by Laura Garrard

Frank Stella: American Abstract Artist
by James Pearson

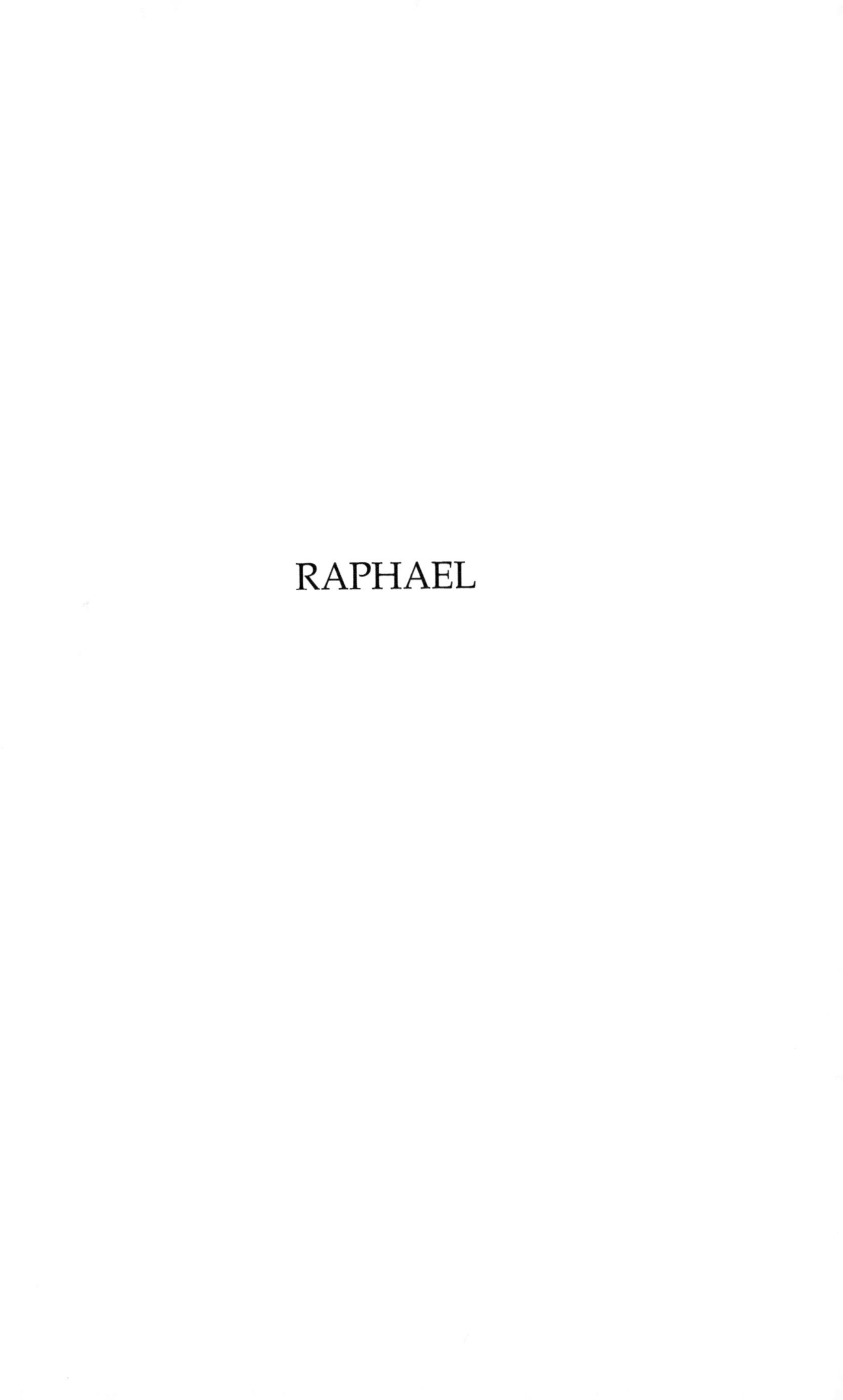

RAPHAEL

RAPHAEL

BY PAUL G. KONODY

CRESCENT MOON

First published in 1908. This edition © 2018.

Printed and bound in the U.S.A.
Set in Book Antiqua 10 on 14pt.
Designed by Radiance Graphics.

Thanks to the authors and publishers quoted.

British Library Cataloguing in Publication data

ISBN-13 9781861716217 (Pbk)
ISBN-13 9781861717313 (Hbk)

CRESCENT MOON PUBLISHING
P.O. Box 1312, Maidstone, Kent, ME14 5XU
Great Britain, www.crmoon.com

CONTENTS

NOTE ON THE TEXT

The text is from *Raphael* by Paul Konody, published by Frederick A. Stokes, New York City, 1908.

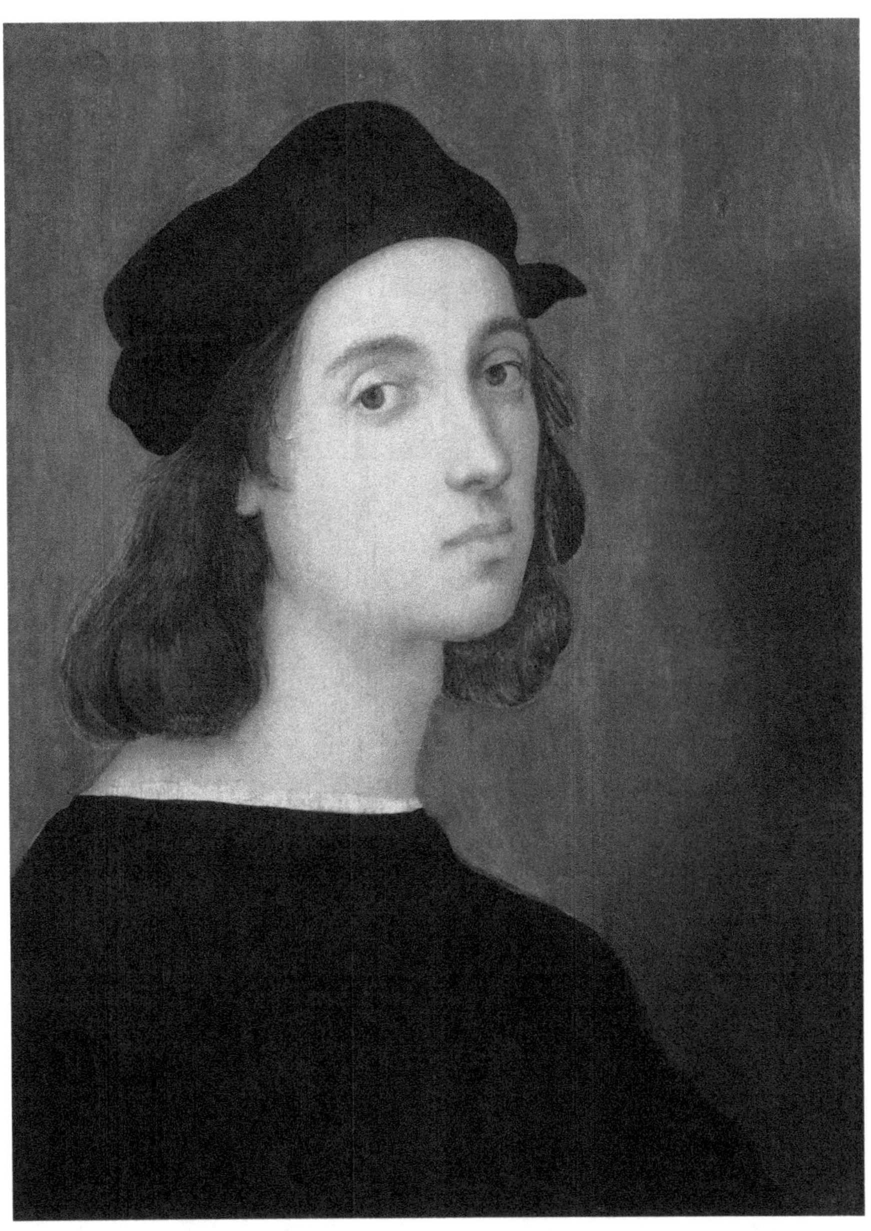

Raphael, Self-Portrait, 1506

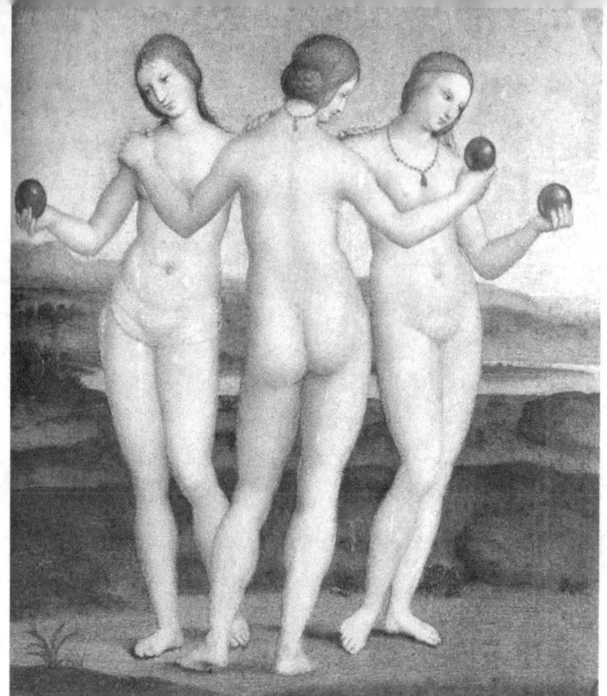

Raphael

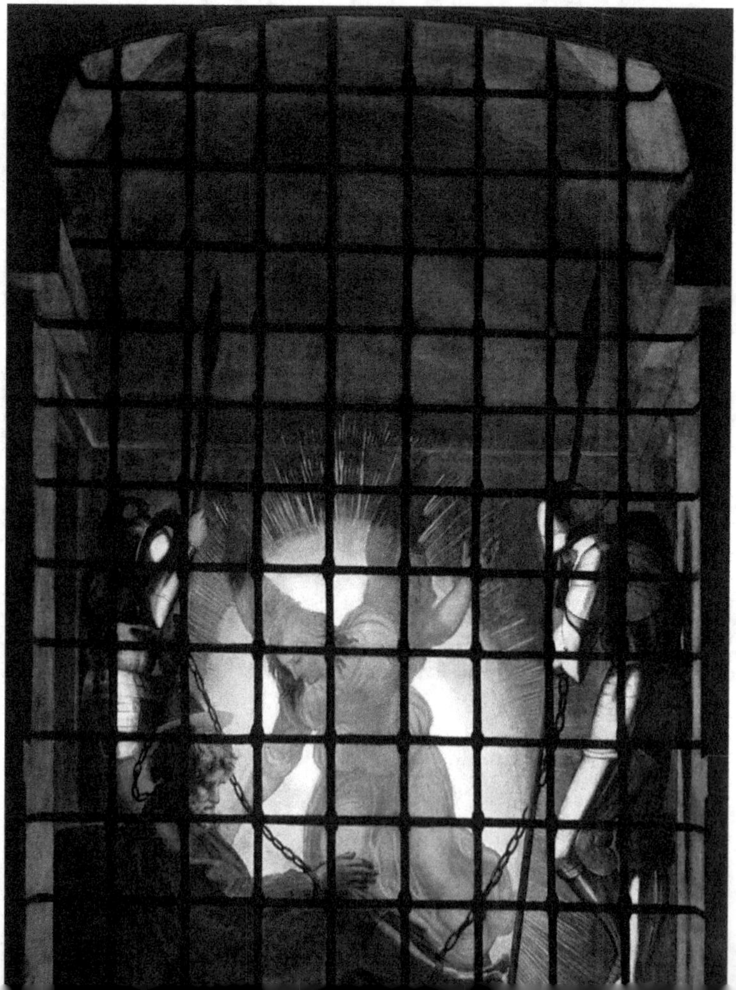

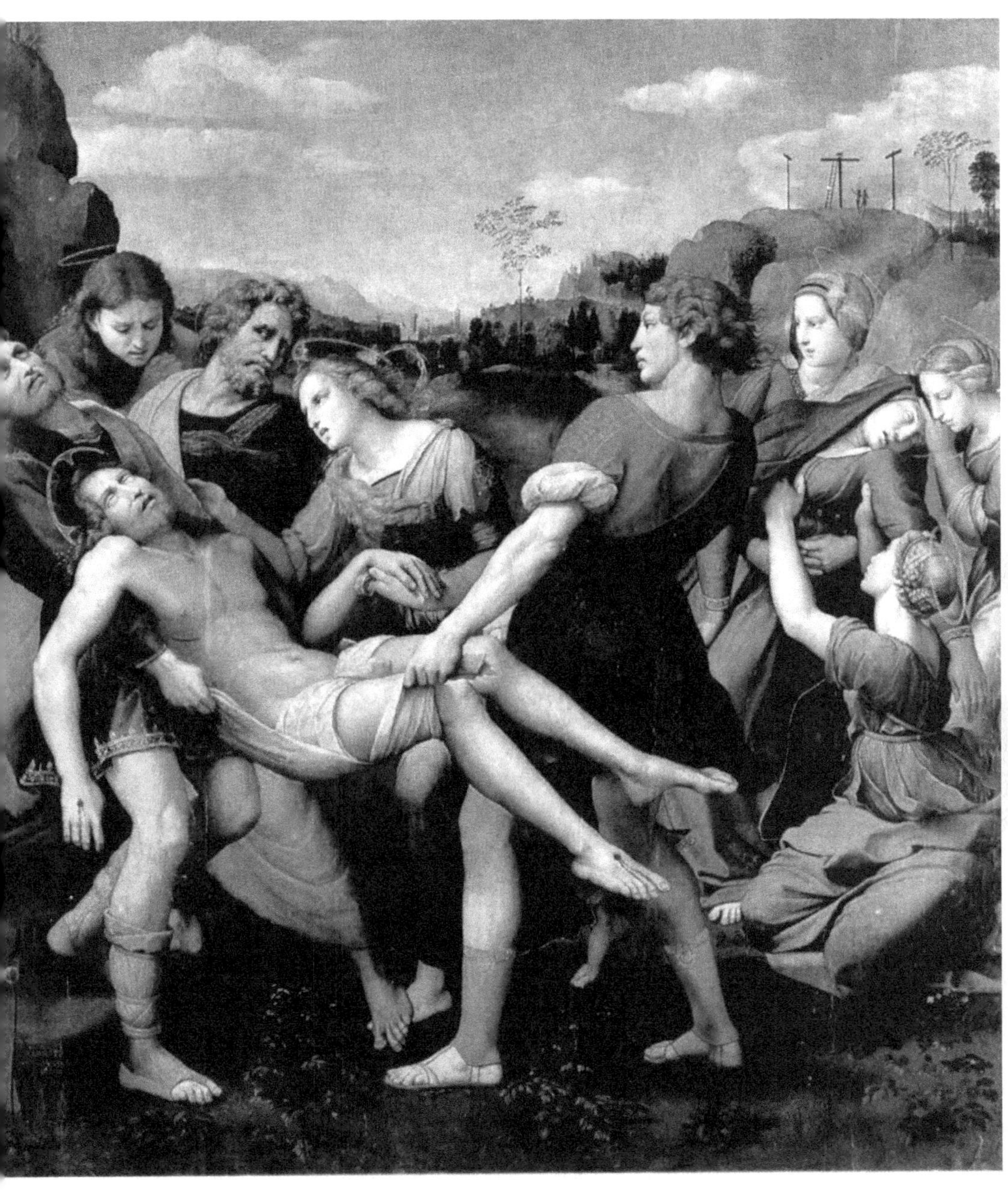

Raphael, The Descent From the Cross, Galleria Borghese, Rome

I

"And I tell you that to paint one beautiful woman, I should need to see several beautiful women, and to have you with me to choose the best," wrote Raphael, then at the zenith of his fame and good fortune, to his life-long friend Count Baldassare Castiglione, who – the ideal courtier himself – has given the world that immortal monument of Renaissance culture, the Book of the Courtier. In penning these lines the prince of painters intended, perhaps, no more than a pretty compliment to one who was himself a model of courtesy and graceful speech, but the words would gain deep significance if *picture* were substituted for *woman,* and if Castiglione were taken to signify the personification of intellect and learning. For the beauty of Raphael's art, which in the course of four centuries has lost none of its hold upon the admiration of mankind, is distilled from the various elements of beauty contained in the art that had gone before him and was being created around him; and in choosing the best, at least as far as idea and conception are concerned, he was guided by the deepest thinkers and keenest intellects of what were then the world's greatest centres of culture.

Raphael was, indeed, born under a happy constellation. He was not a giant of intellect, nor an epoch-making genius; as Michelangelo said of him, he owed his art less to nature than to study; but he was born at a time when two centuries of gradual artistic development had led up to a point where an artist was needed to gather up the diverging threads and bring the movement to a culmination, which will stand for all times as a standard of perfection. Advantages of birth and early surroundings, charm of appearance and disposition which made him a favourite wherever he went, receptivity, adaptability, and application, and above all an early and easy mastery of technique, were combined in Raphael to lead him to this achievement. The smooth unclouded progress of his life from recognition to fame, from prosperity to affluence, is not the turbulent way of genius. Genius walks a sad and lonely path. Michelangelo, the turbulent spirit, morose and dissatisfied, Lionardo da Vinci, pursuing his high ideals without a thought of worldly success until his lonely old age sees him expatriated and contemplating the fruitlessness of all his labours – these men of purest genius have little in common with the pliant courtier Raphael, the head himself of a little court of faithful followers. The story goes that Michelangelo, in the bitterness of his spirit, when meeting his happy rival at the head of his usual army of some fifty dependants on his way to the Papal court, addressed him with the words "You walk like the sheriff with his *posse comitatus.*" And Raphael, quick at repartee, retorted "And you, like an executioner going to the scaffold." Whether the anecdote be true or not, it marks the difference between the course of talent – albeit the rarest talent – and that of genius.

•

What are the qualities of Raphael's art that have carried his fame unsullied through the ages and made him the most popular, the most admired, of all painters? The greatest of the primitives, and of the later masters Velazquez, Rembrandt, Frans Hals, Watteau, to mention only a few of the brightest beacons in the realm of art, have at some time or other been eclipsed and held in slight esteem. Raphael alone escaped the inconstancy of popular favour; he was set up as an idol before he left the world to mourn his untimely death, and in the course of the years the world's idolatrous worship was extended even to the feeble handiwork of his assistants, which often passed under his name. Only within the memory of living men did this blind and indiscriminating worship lead to a reaction as indiscriminating. But this reaction was confined to a comparatively small circle of æsthetically inclined art enthusiasts; and to-day, when the more scientific methods of criticism have succeeded in sifting the wheat from the chaff – the master's own work from the factory-like production of his bottega – he has been reinstated in all his former glory. Contemptuous hostility to Raphael's art has ceased to be a fashionable pose. The frank acknowledgment of the perfection of this art is no longer stayed by the consciousness of the harm done by that imperfect imitation of the Raphaelic code of beauty, which has been the result of all academic teaching in Europe since the founding of the Prix de Rome.

Beauty, formal beauty, pure and faultless, must appeal to everybody; and Raphael means to us the perfection of beauty – such beauty as lies in rhythm, balance, colour, form, and execution. It is a calculated beauty, the lucid, unambiguous expression of an absolutely normal, well-balanced mind assisted by an unerring hand; hence it is intelligible to everybody without that unconscious mental effort which is needed for the understanding of an art of greater emotional intensity. It is of the very essence of art that it should express an emotion; a picture which is merely imitative without holding a hint of what the artist felt at the time of creating it, ceases to be a work of art, even if it represents a subject beautiful in itself. On the other hand, an ugly subject may be raised to sublime art by emotional statement; but this emotion is of necessity more complex and more difficult to understand than that simplest of all emotions, the pleasure caused by the contemplation of beauty. This accounts for the common fallacy that art and beauty are indissolubly connected, and for the favouritism shown by all the successive generations to Raphael whose brush was wedded to beauty in the classic sense, and whose art knew nothing of the beauty of character.

But beauty alone does not constitute Raphael's greatness, or Bouguereau and many other modern academic painters would have to be accounted great instead of being merely dull and insipid. Raphael developed to its utmost power of expressiveness the art of space-composition, the secret of which was the heritage of the Umbrian painters. What space-composition means cannot be better defined than it has been by Mr. Berenson: "Space-composition differs from ordinary composition in the first place most obviously in that it is not an arrangement to be judged as extending only laterally, or up and down on a flat surface, but as extending inwards in depth as well. It is composition in three dimensions, and not in two, in the cube, not merely on the surface.... Painted space-composition opens out the space it frames in, puts boundaries only ideal to the roof of heaven. All that it uses, whether the forms of the natural landscape, or of grand architecture, or even of the human figure, it reduces to be its ministrants in conveying a sense of untrammelled, but not chaotic spaciousness. In such pictures, how freely one breathes – as if a load had just been lifted from one's breast; how refreshed, how noble, how potent one feels; again, how soothed; and still again, how wafted forth to abodes of far-away bliss!"

This sense of space and depth is achieved by methods which have nothing in common with our modern art of creating the illusion of what is called "atmosphere" – not by the "losing and finding" of contours, not by the application of optical theories, such as the zone of interchanging rays which dissolves all hard outlines, nor by the blurring and fogging of the distance. Space-composition in the sense in which it was practised by Raphael is closely akin to the art of architecture in its appeal to our emotions.

As an illustrator, again, Raphael was unequalled as regards clear, direct, measured statement of all that is essential to the immediate grasping of the idea or incident depicted. The first glance at one of Raphael's works, whether it be a small panel picture or a monumental fresco, reveals its whole purport, and that in a manner so complete and lucid and convincing as could not be achieved by any other method of expression. With infallible sureness he invariably found the shortest way for the harmonious statement of idea, form, and emotion, which in his work are always found in perfect balance and so completely permeated by each other as to constitute an indissoluble trinity.

Another reason for Raphael's powerful appeal – and in this he is perhaps the most typical child of his period – is that his art unites in one majestic current the two greatest movements of thought which have ever fired the imagination of civilised Europe; classic antiquity and Christian faith, when treated by Raphael's brush, cease to be incompatible and live side by side in that measured harmony which is the hall-mark of his art. Christianity is presented to us in the glorious classic garb of the old world, and the myth and philosophy of the ancients are brought into intimate relationship with Christian teaching. He infuses new blood and life into the stones of ancient Greece and Rome – unlike Mantegna who had remained cold and classic in his relief-like reconstructions of antiquity; just as he accentuates the human emotional side of the Madonna and Child *motif* by discarding all hieroglyphic symbolism and setting before our eyes the intimate link of love that connects mother and babe. Almost imperceptibly his cupids are transformed into child angels, and the Jehovah of his "Vision of Ezekiel" has more in common with Olympian Jove than with the mediæval conception of the Lord of Heaven.

Just as Timoteo Viti, Perugino, Fra Bartolommeo, Lionardo da Vinci, Masaccio, Michelangelo, and Sebastiano del Piombo (who imparted to him something of the glow of Venetian colouring), had been the sources from which Raphael drew his knowledge of technique, colour, composition, and all the elements of pictorial style, so the humanists had paved his way as regards the intellectual aspect of his art. His marvellous faculty of rapid assimilation enabled him, on the one hand, to appropriate whatever he found worthy of imitation in his precursors and contemporaries, and thus to complete his technical equipment at an age at which it was given to few to have achieved mastery; whilst, on the other hand, his clear intellect, aided by the not entirely unmercenary desire to please his patrons, helped him to carry out with triumphant success the ideas evolved by the keenest thinkers of his time. To doubt that the general idea, and perhaps a good many of the details, of such a stupendous work as the fresco decoration of the *Stanze* at the Vatican, had originated in Raphael's head, is not to detract from his greatness. He was a boy in his early teens when he entered his first master's bottega. He was a youth of twenty-five when he started on his great task; and the intervening years had been so completely filled with the study of his craft and with the execution of important commissions, that it is impossible to believe he could have found much leisure for book-learning. And such learning was indispensable for the conception of that elaborate scheme with all its historical allusions and allegorical imagery. The wonder is that Raphael could so completely enter into the suggestions made to him from various sources, and to weave them into a tissue of immortal beauty.

II

At the end of the fifteenth century the rule of the Duke Federigo of Montefeltre, an enlightened prince who devoted the best of his energy and such time as he could spare from his duties on the battlefield to the patronage of the arts, to the adornment of his noble palace, and to the collecting of priceless manuscripts, paintings, antiques, and works of art of every description, had raised the old city of Urbino to one of the centres of culture and learning, and made the ducal court a gathering-place for the distinguished painters, architects, poets, and humanists who were attracted by the wealth and liberality of this great patron. Among the less distinguished satellites attracted by the sun of Montefeltre was one Giovanni Santi, who had come to Urbino in the middle of the fifteenth century. Though a painter of considerable skill, trained perhaps by Fiorenzo di Lorenzo, he found it necessary in the early days of his sojourn at Urbino to supplement his modest income by trading in oil and corn and other commodities, as his father had done before him. But his varied accomplishments soon brought him into prominence and secured him a position as court painter and poet. More important than any of the pictures that have come to us from his brush is his famous rhyming chronicle of 23,000 verses in Dantesque measure, in which he glorifies the virtues and exploits of his patron. He was a special favourite of Elisabetta Gonzaga, the youthful spouse of Federigo's son

Guidobaldo, whose high esteem for Giovanni is expressed in a letter in which she informs her sister-in-law of the court painter's death.

To this Giovanni Santi and to his wife Magia Ciarla was born on Good Friday, the 28th of March[1] 1483, a son who was destined in the comparatively short span of his life to rise to fame such as has been the share of few mortals. An elder brother and sister of Raphael had died in infancy, and his mother followed them to the grave before he had reached his eighth year. Her place in the paternal home was taken by Bernardina Parte, a goldsmith's daughter, whom Giovanni wedded soon after his first wife's death. From Giovanni Santi's great poem it would appear that he was on terms of friendship and intimacy with some of the greatest masters of the time, such as Melozzo da Forli, Mantegna, Pier dei Franceschi, and Verrocchio; and it is reasonable to assume that Raphael's earliest art education under his father's guidance tended towards the development of that peculiar faculty which enabled him later on to seize and assimilate the excellences in the style of the various masters with whom he came in contact.

The ease with which his precocious talent absorbed the teaching of his masters became evident when, soon after his father's death, in 1494, from fever contracted in the malarial air of the Mantuan marshland, whither he had gone in the service of Elisabetta Gonzaga, he entered the bottega of Francia's pupil Timoteo Viti (or della Vite), who settled at Urbino in 1495, and whose eminent position among the painters of that city must have suggested to Raphael's guardian – his maternal uncle Simone Ciarla – the desirability of placing the youth under such competent tuition. And so thoroughly did Raphael acquire not only his first master's style, but even such of his mannerisms as the broad shape of hands and feet and the languid turn of the heads, that from such internal evidence Morelli, the originator of

---

1 The wording of Raphael's epitaph, which states that he died on the same day (of the year) on which he was born, has led some writers to the assumption that he was born on April 6, whereas it is merely meant to signify that he was born and died on Good Friday.

the modern method of criticism, was able after more than three centuries of error to disprove Vasari's assertion that Raphael passed straight from his father's workshop into that of Perugino. Timoteo's influence is apparent even in works painted by Raphael at a time when he had come under the spell of the more powerful personality of Perugino, like the "Sposalizio" or "Betrothal of the Virgin," of 1504, in the Brera Gallery in Milan; but it is unmistakably in evidence in the three earliest pictures that bear Raphael's name: the "Vision of a Knight," at the National Gallery, the "St. Michael," at the Louvre, and the "Three Graces," at Chantilly. Not only the features which connect this group of pictures with the style of Timoteo Viti, but the timid meticulous execution and the naïve stiffness of the figures, mark them as works of Raphael's immature youth. The turn of the century, as we shall see, found Raphael at Perugia, so that the three pictures mentioned must have been painted before he had attained the age of seventeen. The panel of the "Three Graces," which, by the way, was obviously inspired by an antique cameo, was bought in 1885 by the Duc d'Aumale from Lord Dudley's collection for £25,000 – surely a price without parallel for a work painted by a lad of sixteen! A portrait in chalk of the marvellously gifted, winsome boy by the hand of his first master is preserved at the University Galleries in Oxford.

The records of a lawsuit between some members of his family prove that Raphael was still at Urbino in 1499, since in the summer of this year he appeared as a witness in court. When the verdict was given in the following year, he had already left for Perugia to continue his studies as an assistant of Perugino. Again we find him before long assimilating the style of his new master so successfully and completely that, to use Vasari's words, "His copies cannot be distinguished from the original works of the master, nor can the difference between the performances of Raphael and those of Pietro be discerned with any certainty." Plagiarism in those days did not trouble the artistic conscience, and it is easy to trace in Raphael's pictures of that period entire groups that are borrowed from the elder master. Thus the "Crucifixion," painted about 1501 for a church in Città di Castello, and now in the collection of Dr. Ludwig Mond, is obviously based on Perugino's version of the same subject at St. Augustine's, Siena, whilst the whole upper part of the Vatican "Coronation of the Virgin" is "lifted" from an "Assumption" by Pietro. But this almost literal imitation was only a passing phase, whilst the great lesson of space-composition and the typically Umbrian gift of almost religious fervour in stating the peaceful glory of the Umbrian hill-land, which had been imparted to Raphael at Perugia, remained permanent acquisitions to his art.

•

In 1502 Perugino went back to Florence, and Raphael probably joined Pinturicchio's staff of assistants, though Vasari's statement that he furnished the designs for the latter master's frescoes in the Piccolomini Library at Siena may be dismissed as a fable. During this time Raphael painted his first Madonna pictures, notably the "Conestabile Madonna" (now at St. Petersburg), which is based entirely on Perugino's "Virgin with the Pomegranate," and two panels at the Berlin Museum. The Milan "Sposalizio," in which the young master's personality already asserts itself through the very marked Ferrarese and Peruginesque influences, was painted in 1504 for the church of St. Francesco at Città di Castello. His early mastery in portraiture is illustrated by his portrait of Perugino at the Borghese Gallery, which is so firm in character and perfect in execution that it could pass for many years as the handiwork of Holbein.

Meanwhile Duke Guidobaldo had returned to Urbino after the death of his enemy, Pope Alexander VI., and thither Raphael proceeded in 1504. The little "St. George" at the Louvre is a memento of this short visit which terminated in October of the same year, when Raphael, armed with a letter of warmest recommendation from Guidobaldo's sister Giovanna della Rovere to the Gonfaloniere Pier Soderini, left his native town for Florence, then the centre of artistic life, astir with the rivalry between the giants Michelangelo and Lionardo da Vinci.

The young man must have been fairly bewildered at the multitude of new impressions that crowded upon him in the glorious city on the banks of the Arno, with its imposing palaces and churches, its seething life and its art so much more virile and monumental than the dreamy, almost effeminate art engendered by the soft balmy atmosphere of Umbria. How he must have revelled in the contemplation of Masaccio's noble frescoes in the Brancacci Chapel – the training school of generations of painters – which ten years later were echoed in his tapestry cartoons for the Sistine Chapel! How he must have stood in wonder and amazement before Michelangelo's "David," and have resolved forthwith to devote himself to a more intimate study of the human form and movement! The fascination exercised upon him by the genius of Lionardo found expression in some of the earliest fruits of Raphael's sojourn in Florence – the portraits at the Pitti Palace known as "Angelo Doni" and his wife Maddalena Strozzi, who, however, could not possibly have been the model for this reminiscence of Lionardo's "Mona Lisa," since it is known that she was baptized in 1489, whereas Raphael's portrait of 1504 represents a woman of ripe age.

In the workshop of the architect Baccio d'Agnolo, which was then a favourite social resort of the younger artists of Florence, the youth from Urbino met on terms of equality such masters as Ridolfo Ghirlandajo, Antonio da Sangallo, Sansovino, and Fra Bartolommeo, who again had a considerable share in the formation of Raphael's style, as may be seen from the "Madonna di Sant'Antonio," now lent to the National Gallery by Mr. Pierpont Morgan who is said to have paid for it the enormous price of £100,000. This picture, and the "Ansidei Madonna," which was bought for the National Gallery from the Duke of Marlborough's collection for £70,000, were painted during a visit to Perugia towards the end of 1505 – the former for the nuns of St. Antony of Padua, in Perugia, and the other for the Ansidei Chapel in the church of San Fiorenzo of the same city.

•

The records of Raphael's movements between 1504 and 1508, when he finally left Florence, are scanty and unreliable. Certain it is that, besides his visit to Perugia, he spent some time at Urbino in 1506, when he painted for Guidobaldo the "St. George" which figured among the gifts taken by Castiglione to Henry VII. of England, from whom the Duke of Urbino had received the insignia of the Garter two years previously. The picture is now at the Hermitage in St. Petersburg. The majority of those exquisite Madonna pictures, which have contributed more than anything else to Raphael's undying fame and popularity, date from his Florentine period – the "Madonna del Granduca" at the Pitti Palace, the "Casa Tempi Madonna" at Munich, the Chantilly "Madonna of the House of Orleans," the "Madonna of the Meadow" in Vienna, the "Madonna of the Goldfinch" at the Uffizi, the "Madonna of the Lamb" at Madrid, Lord Cowper's famous picture at Panshanger, and the "Belle Jardinière" at the Louvre.

To the same period belongs the portrait of himself, in the Painter's Hall of the Uffizi, and the portrait of a youth in the Budapest National Gallery. On the occasion of his visit to Perugia, Atalanta Baglione, the mother of Grifonetto Baglione who had fallen a victim to the bloody family feud that turned Perugia into a slaughter-house in 1500, commissioned from Raphael an altarpiece in memory of that event – the "Entombment" which the master finished in Florence in 1507, and which is now at the Borghese Gallery. It was Raphael's first attempt at dramatic composition, the art of which he had yet to master – its forced, unnatural emotion lays it more open to criticism than any other work from his own hand.

A law-case in connection with the payment of 100 crowns due by him for a house he had purchased from the Cervasi family, necessitated Raphael's presence at Urbino once again in October 1507. In April of the following year Guidobaldo died; and a letter from Raphael to his uncle Simone Ciarla, who had informed him of this sad event, proves that the master was then back again in Florence. After expressing his grief at the news of the Duke's death ("I could not read your letter without tears"), Raphael appeals in this letter to his uncle to procure him another letter of recommendation to the Gonfaloniere of Florence "from my Lord the Prefect," since it was in the power of the chief magistrate of Florence to place an important commission for the decoration of a certain apartment.

But a better fate was in store for the youthful applicant, who was to be called to a wider field of action. According to Vasari it was Raphael's kinsman, Bramante of Urbino, who drew Pope Julius II.'s attention to the rare gifts of Raphael, and caused him to be summoned to Rome. And the voice of Bramante, who stood in high favour with the Pope, and was engaged on the scheme of rebuilding the Cathedral of St. Peter, would certainly have commanded attention. But on this, as on many other points, Vasari is not wholly trustworthy. First of all, Bramante was not connected with Raphael by any family ties; and, then, it is far more probable that the thought of calling Raphael to Rome to assist in the decoration of the papal apartments in the Vatican was suggested to Julius II. by the Prefetessa Giovanna della Rovere, who had always been a staunch supporter of the Urbinate, or by her son Francesco, the nephew and successor of Duke Guidobaldo Montefeltre. Bramante, who was on terms of friendship with his fellow-artist and fellow-townsman, may well have supported the recommendation. However this may be, Raphael received the Pope's command, and journeyed to Rome, whither he had already been preceded by Michelangelo.

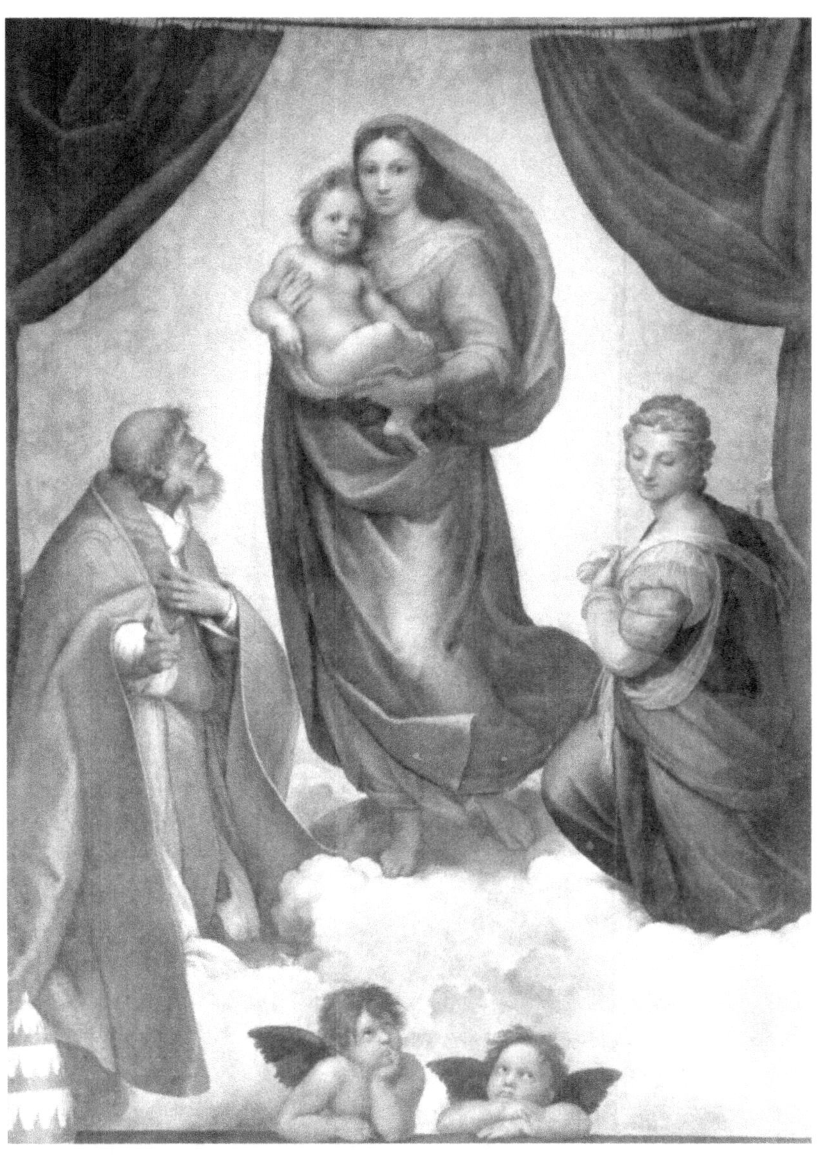

Raphael, Sistine Madonna, 1513-14, Dresden

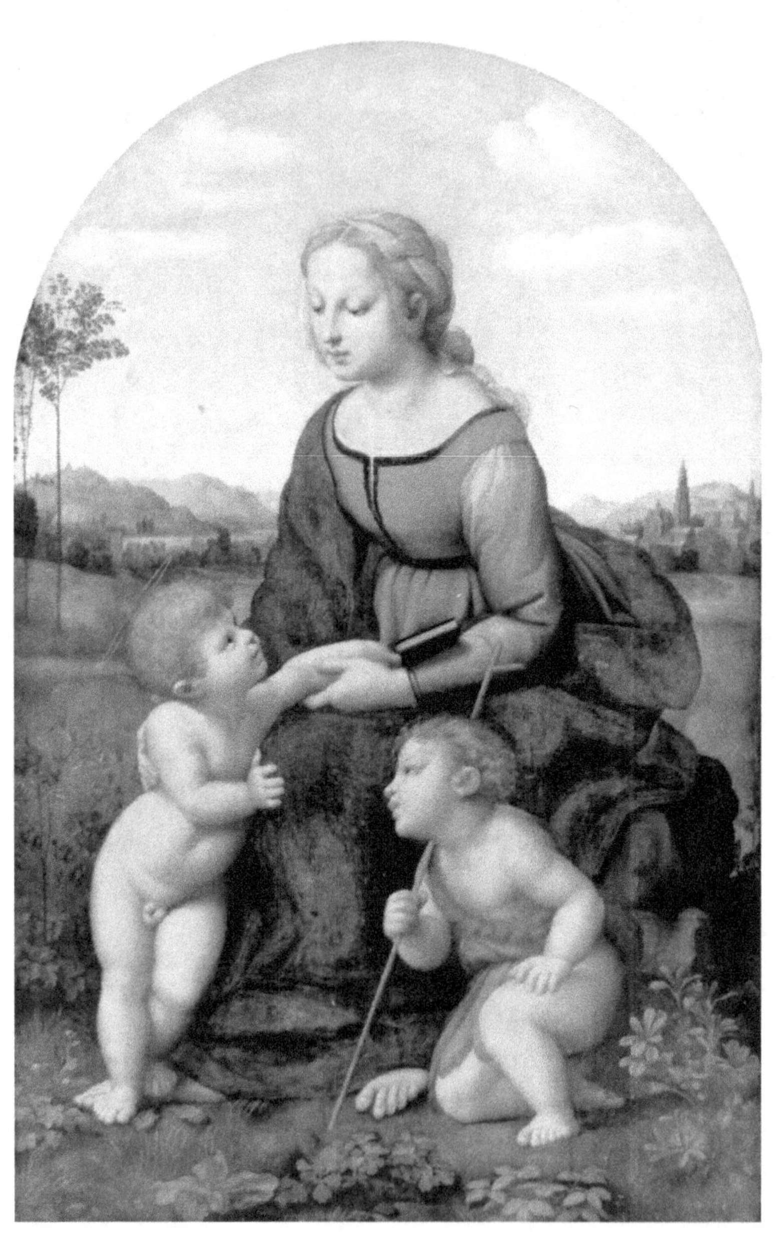

Raphael, La Belle Jardiniere, 1507, Louvre

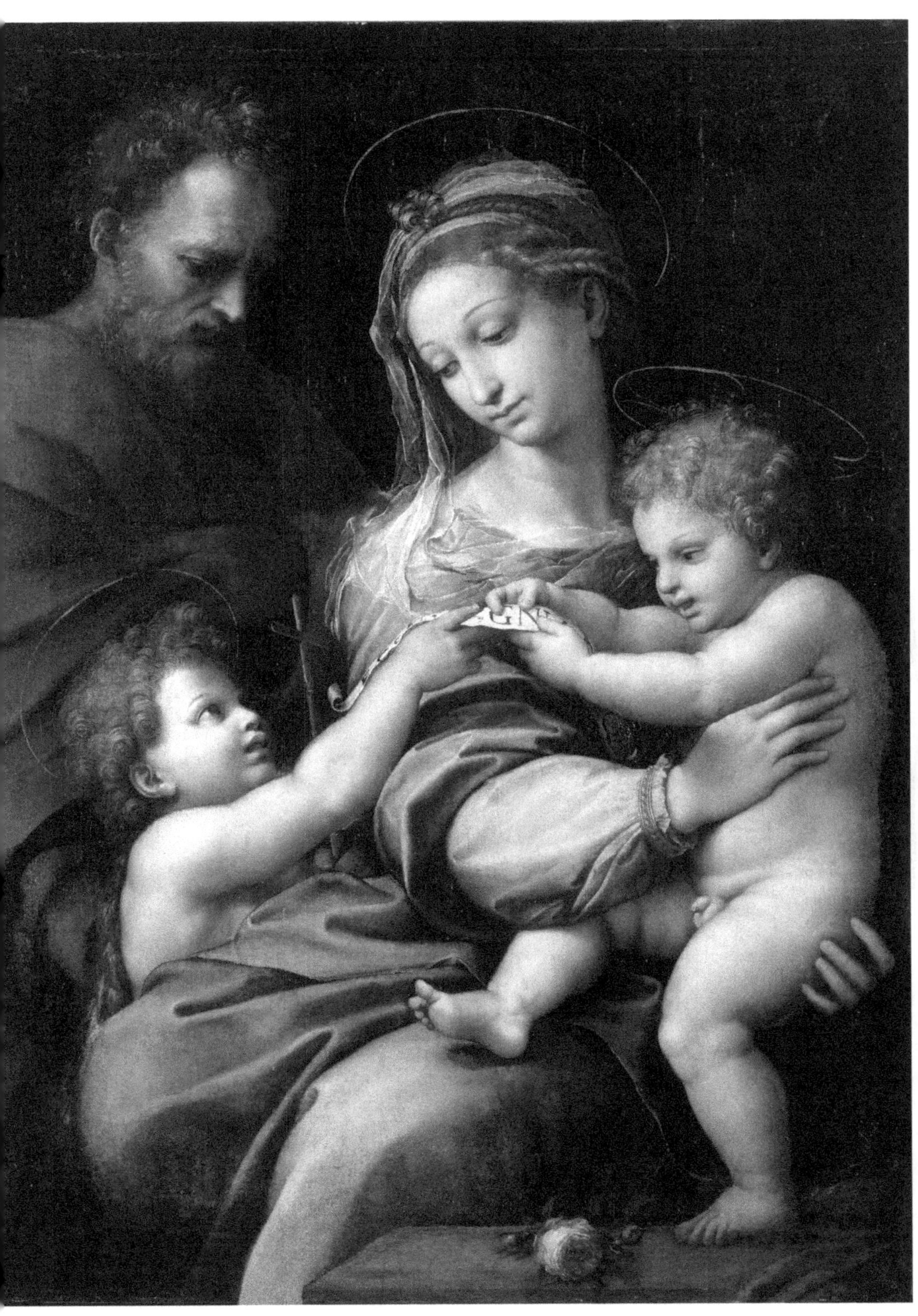

Raphael, Madonna della Rosa, 1517, Prado

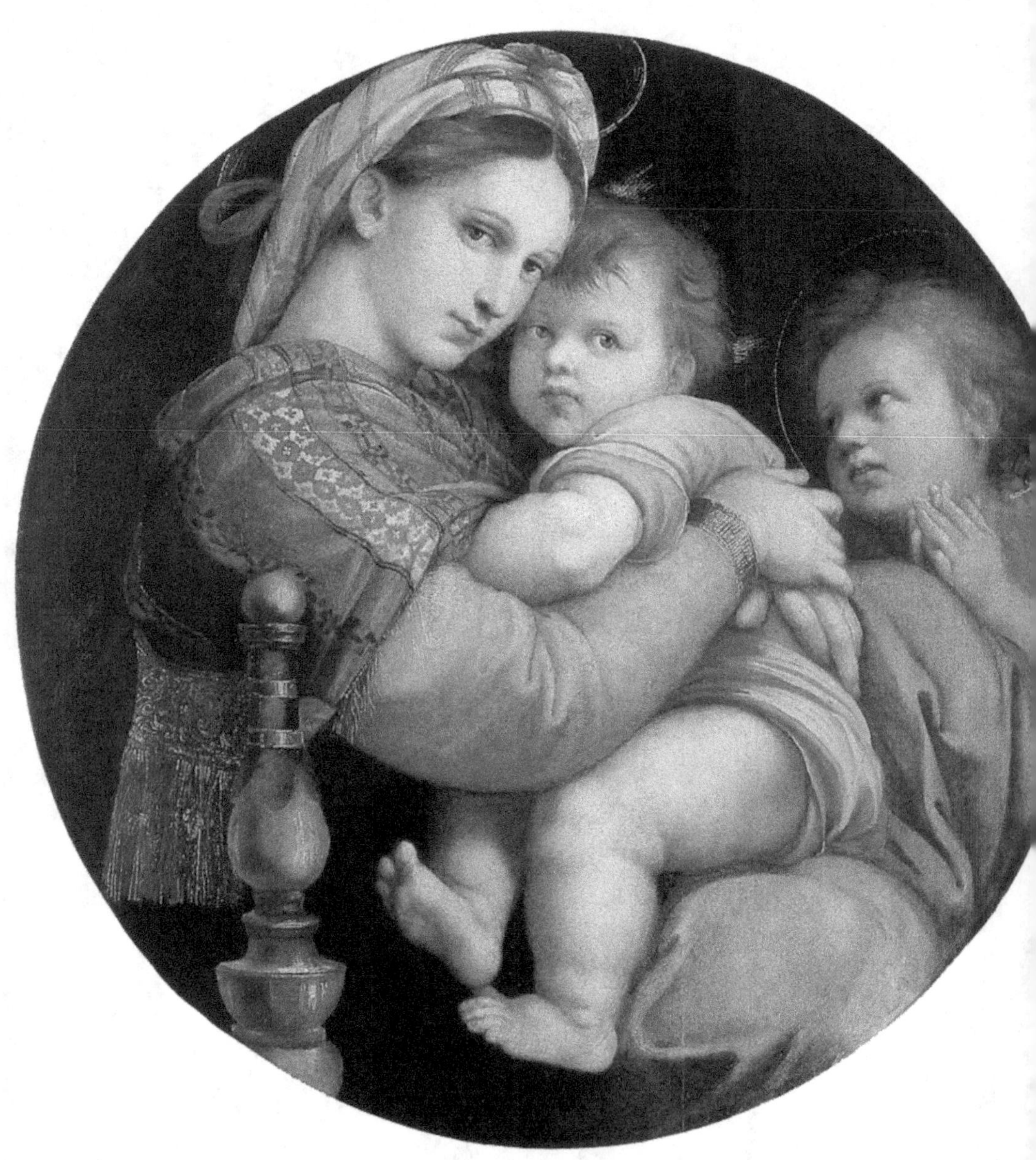

Raphael, Madonna della Seggiola, 1514, Pitti Palace

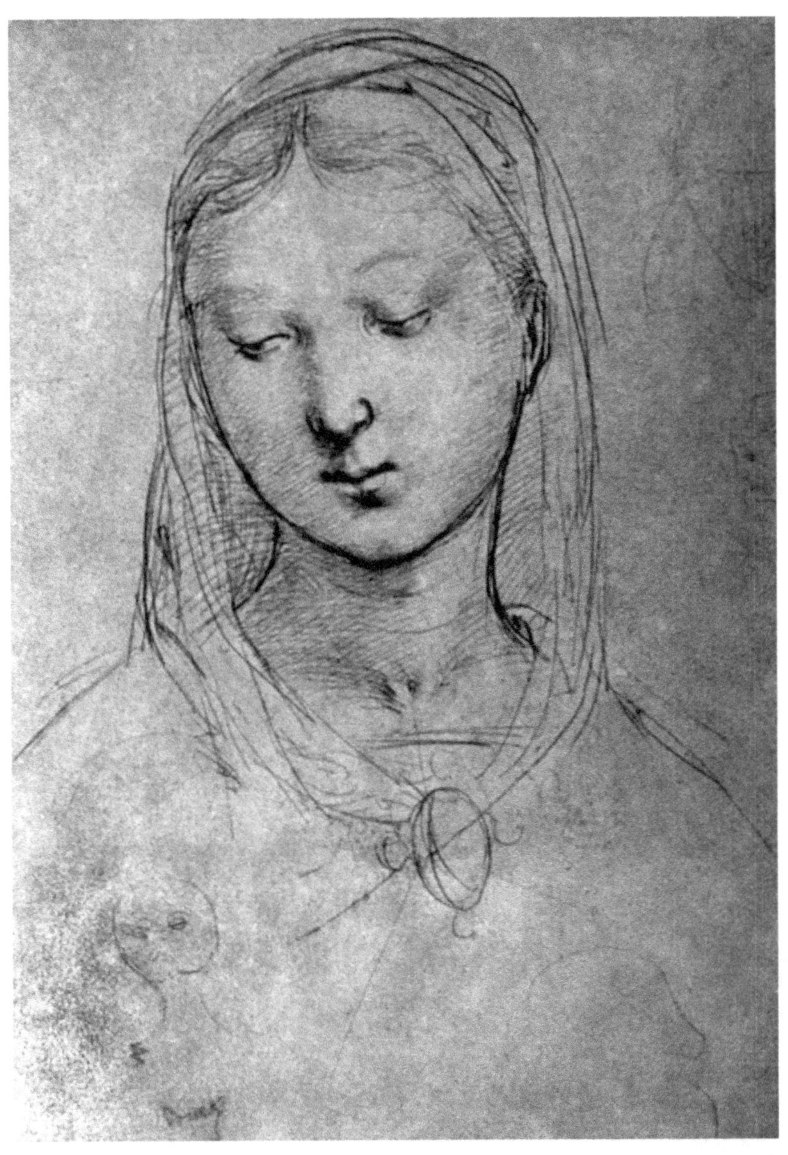

Raphael, Study For the Madonna Solly, 1501, British Museum

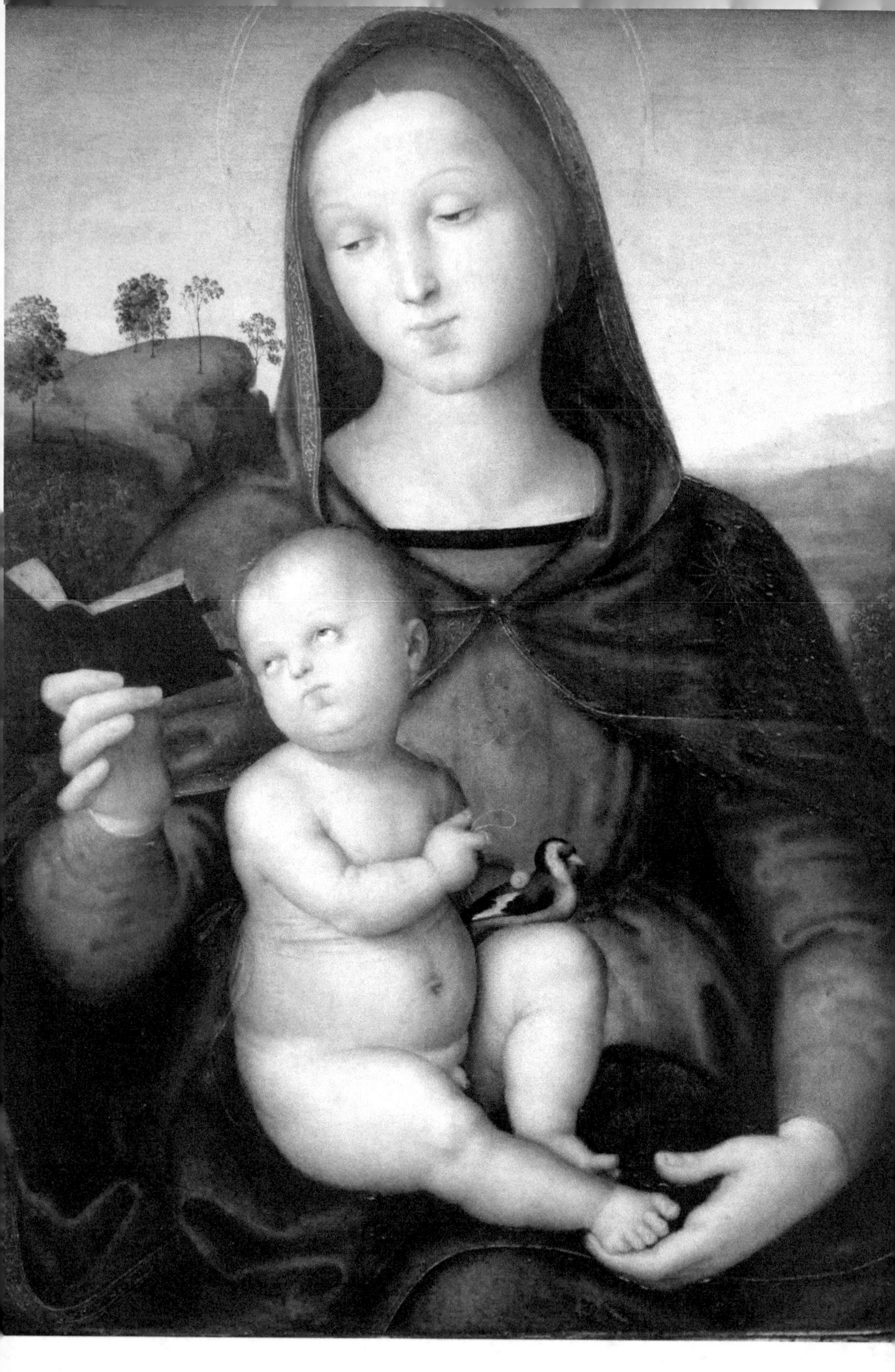

Raphael, Madonna Solly, 1502-03, Berlin

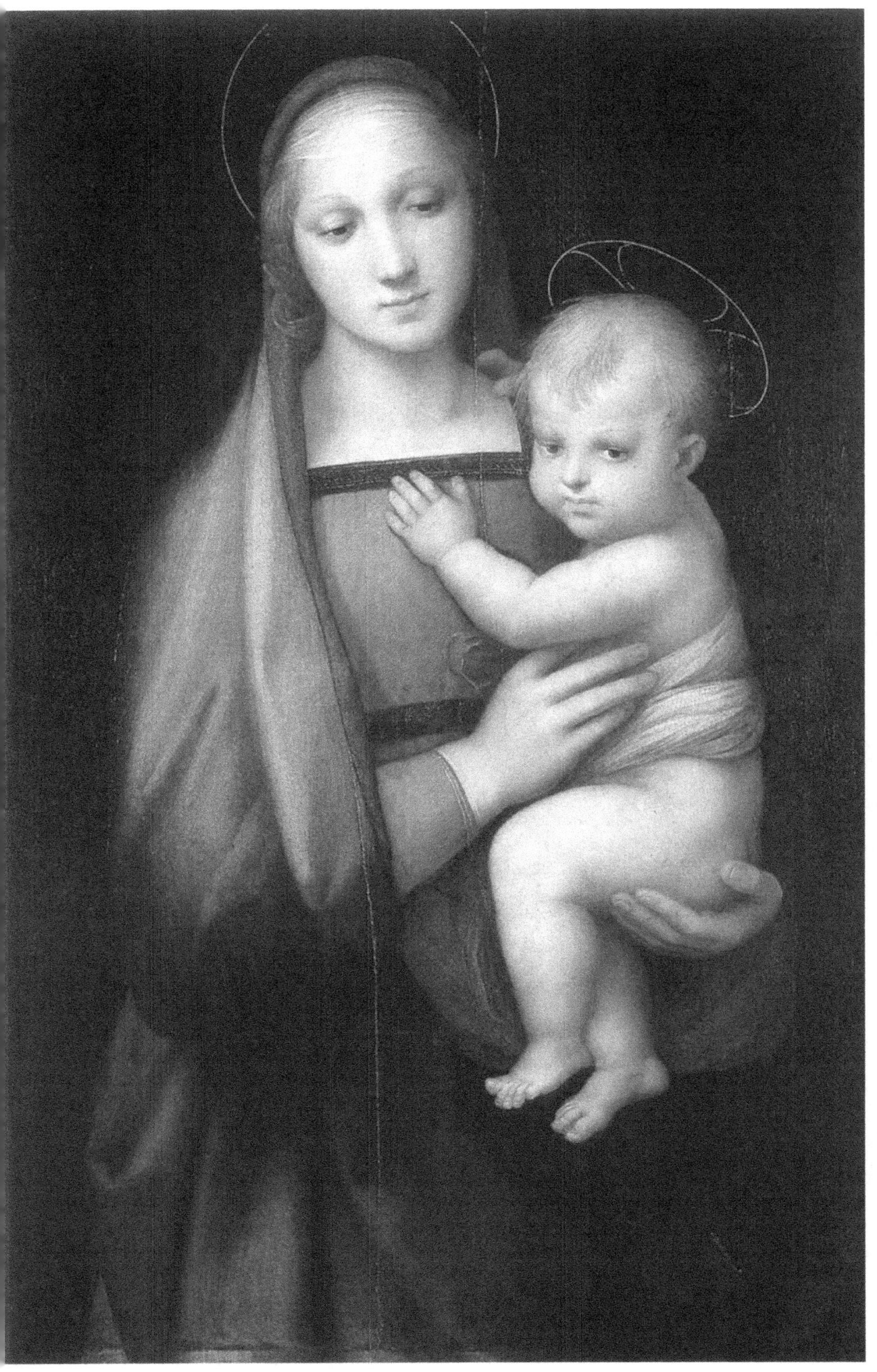

Raphael, Granduca Madonna, 1504, Pitti Palace

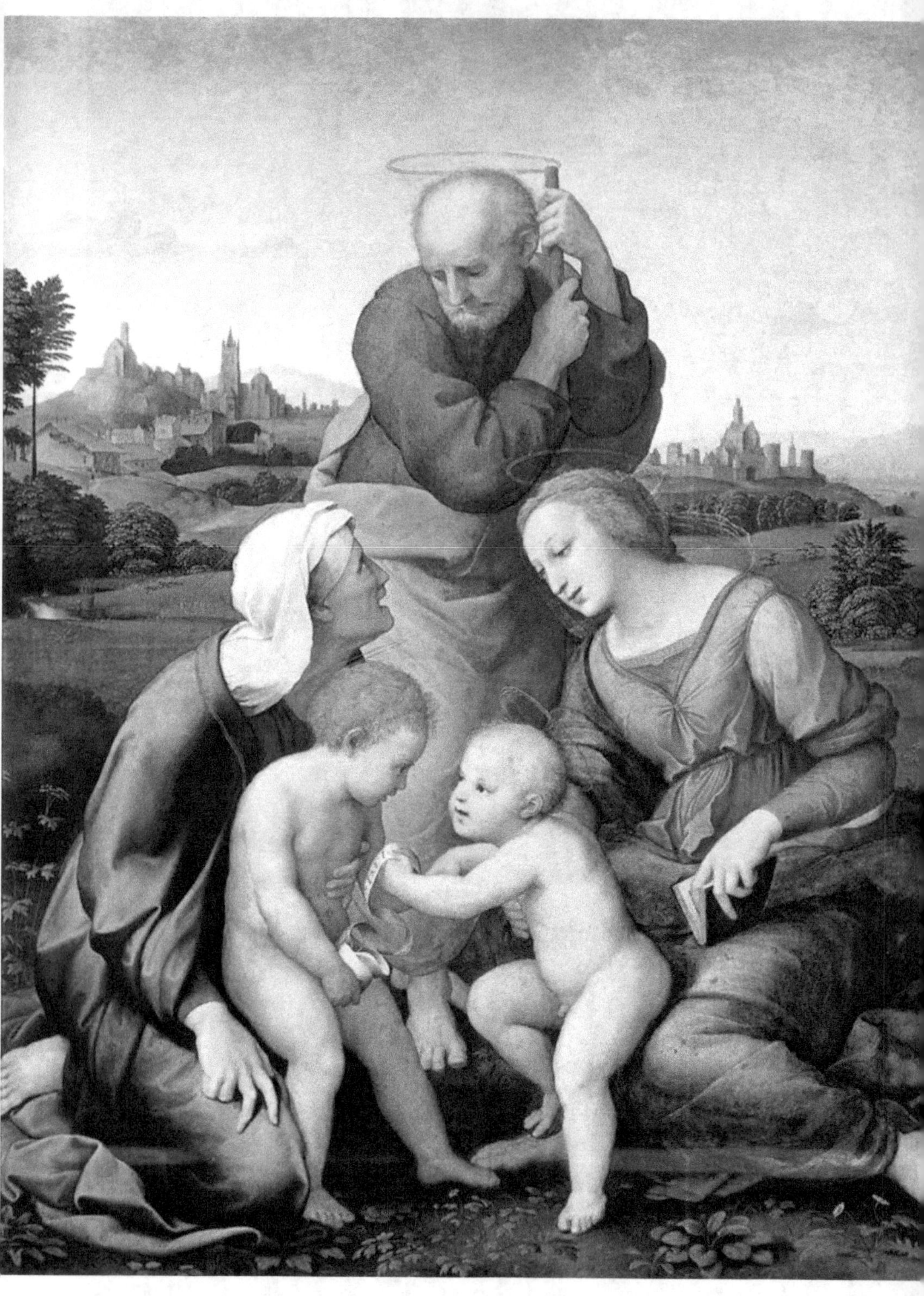

Raphael, The Holy Family, c. 1506, Alte Pinakothek, Munich

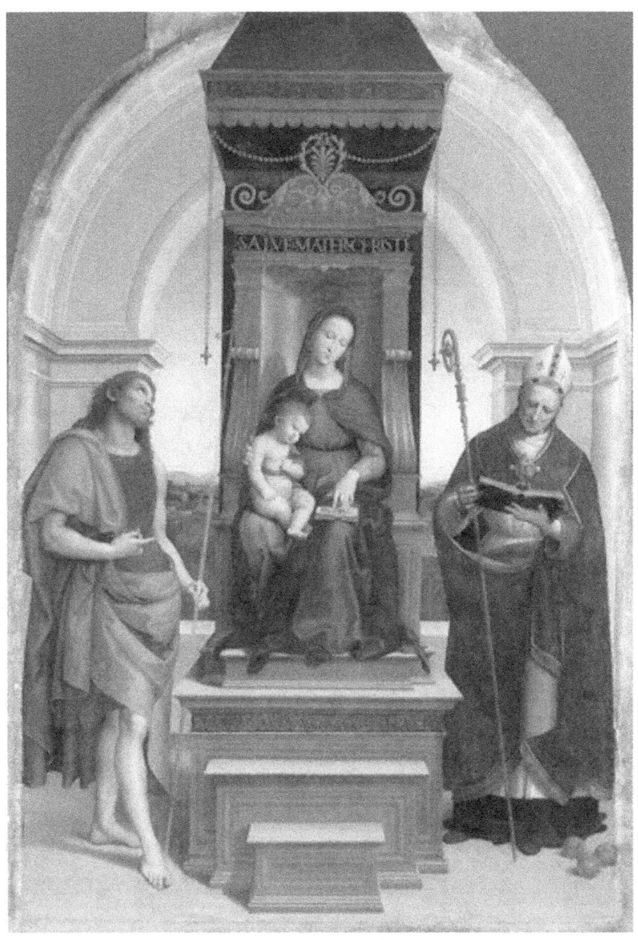

Raphael, The Ansidei Madonna,
National Gallery, London

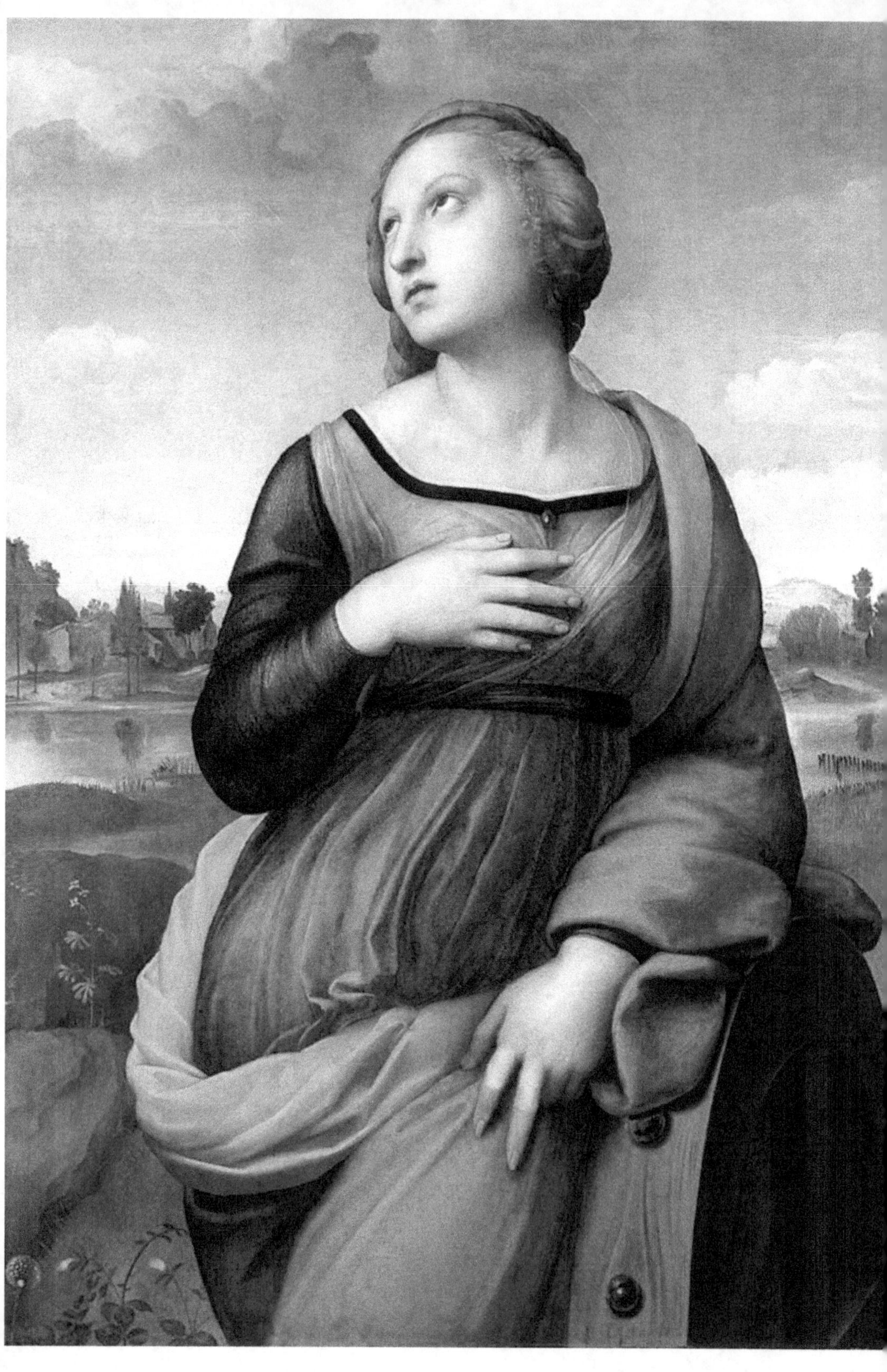

Raphael, St Catherine, 1508, National Gallery, London

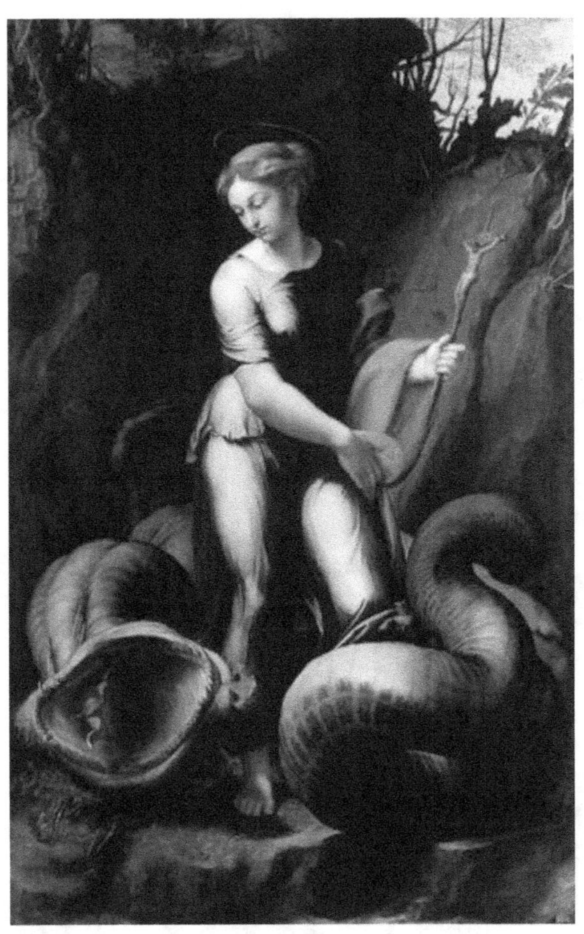

Raphael, St Margaret, 1518, Vienna

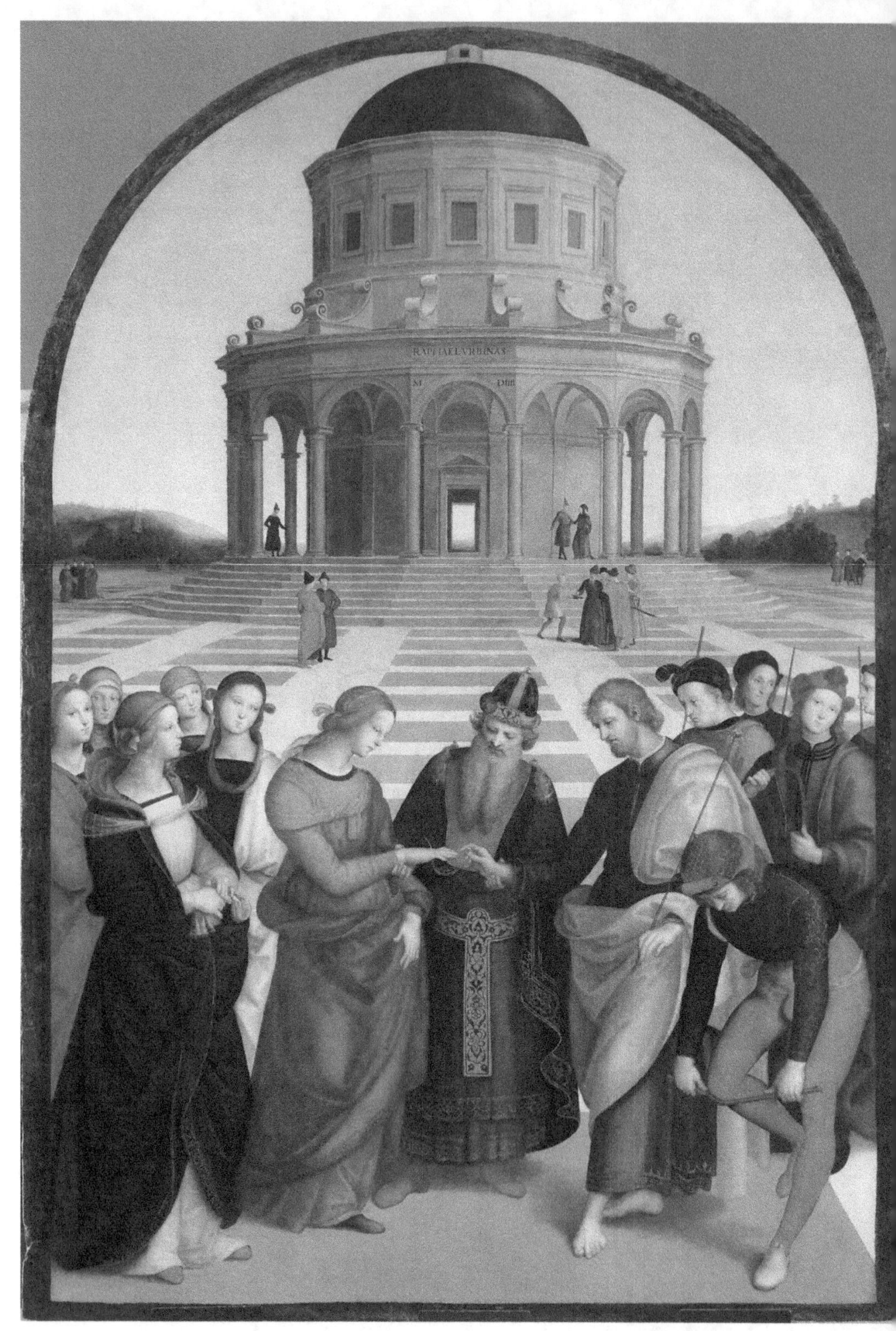

Raphael, The Marriage of the Virgin, 1504, Milan

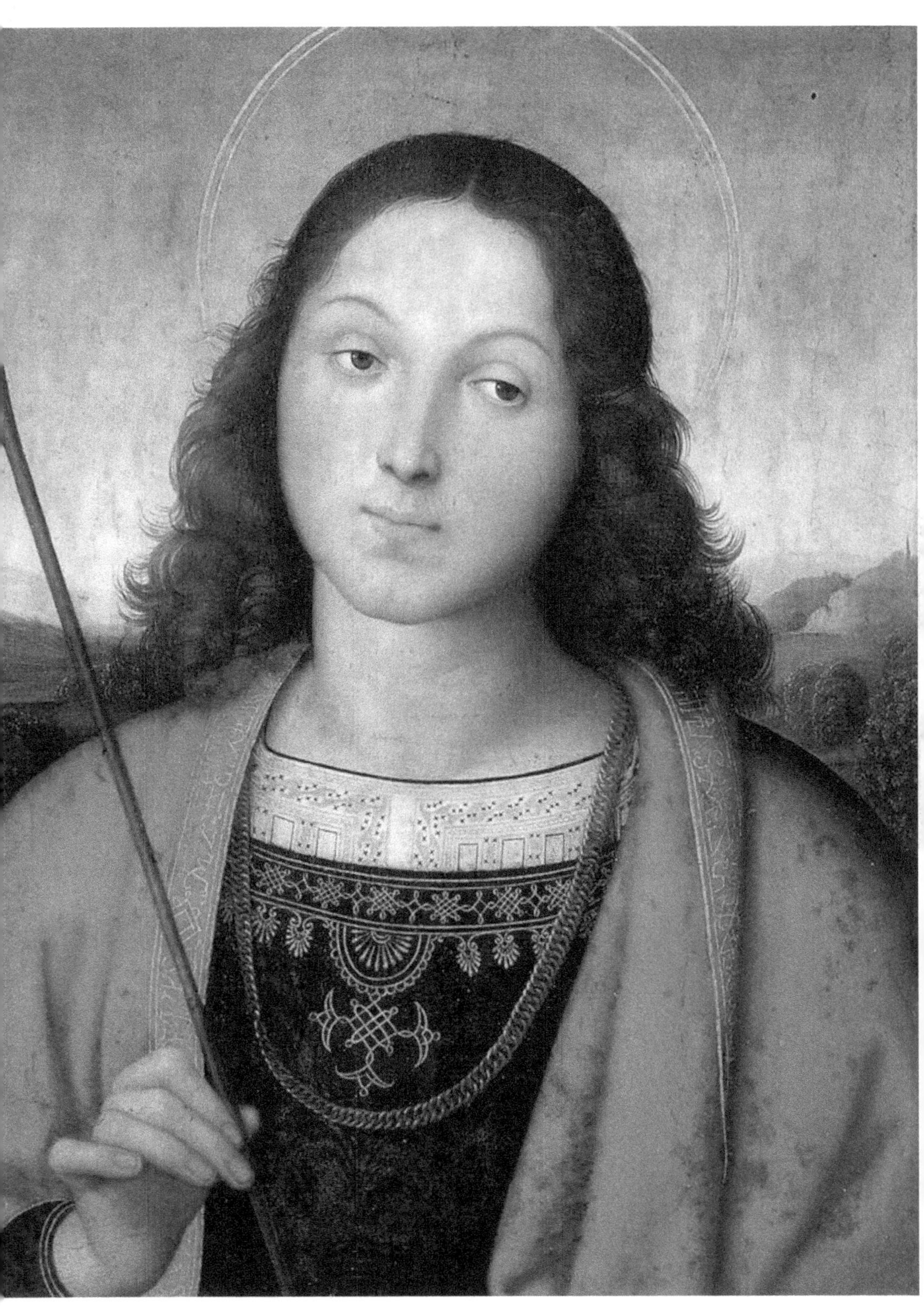

Raphael, St Sebastian, Bergamo

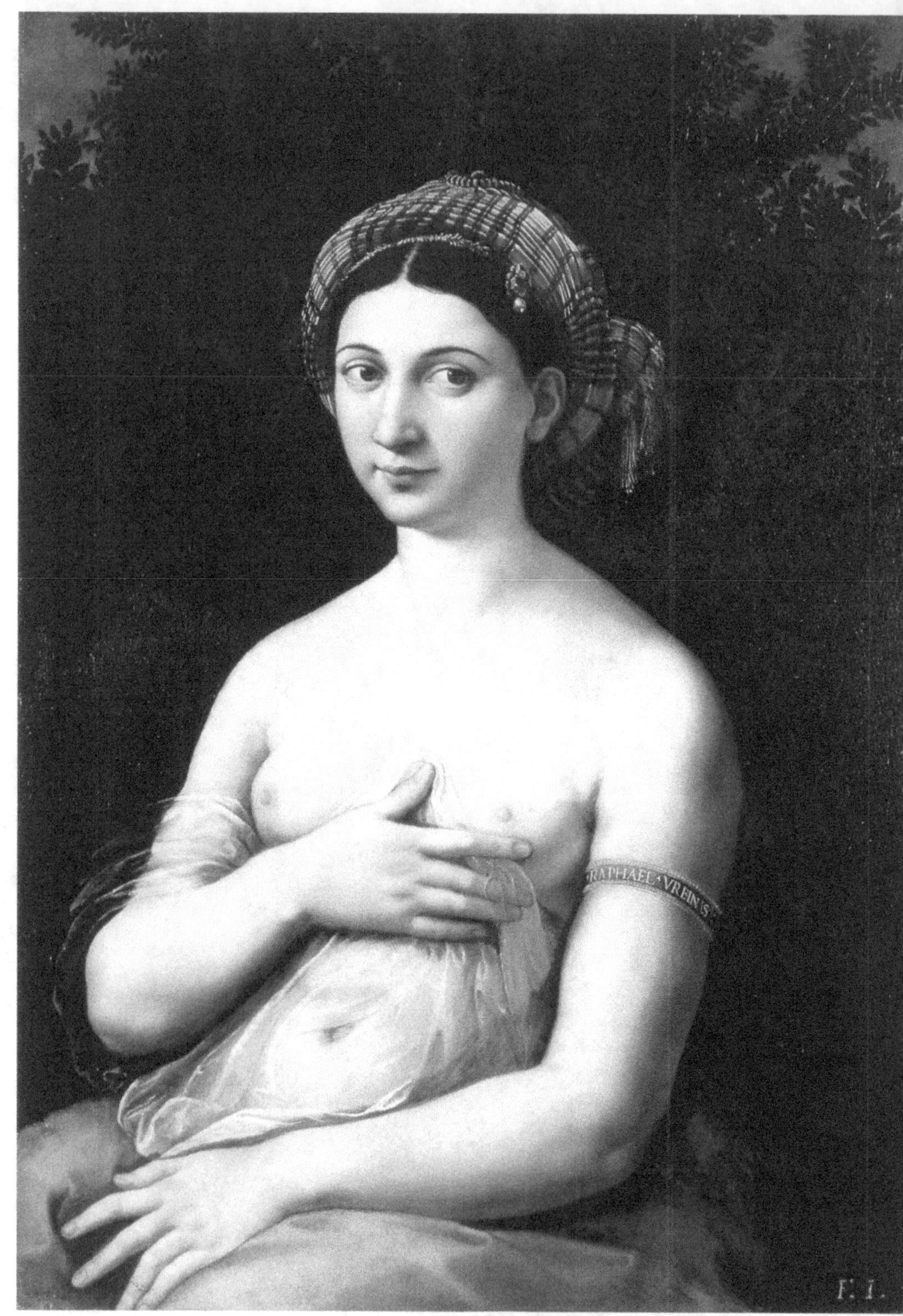

Raphael, La Fornarina, 1515-19, Rome

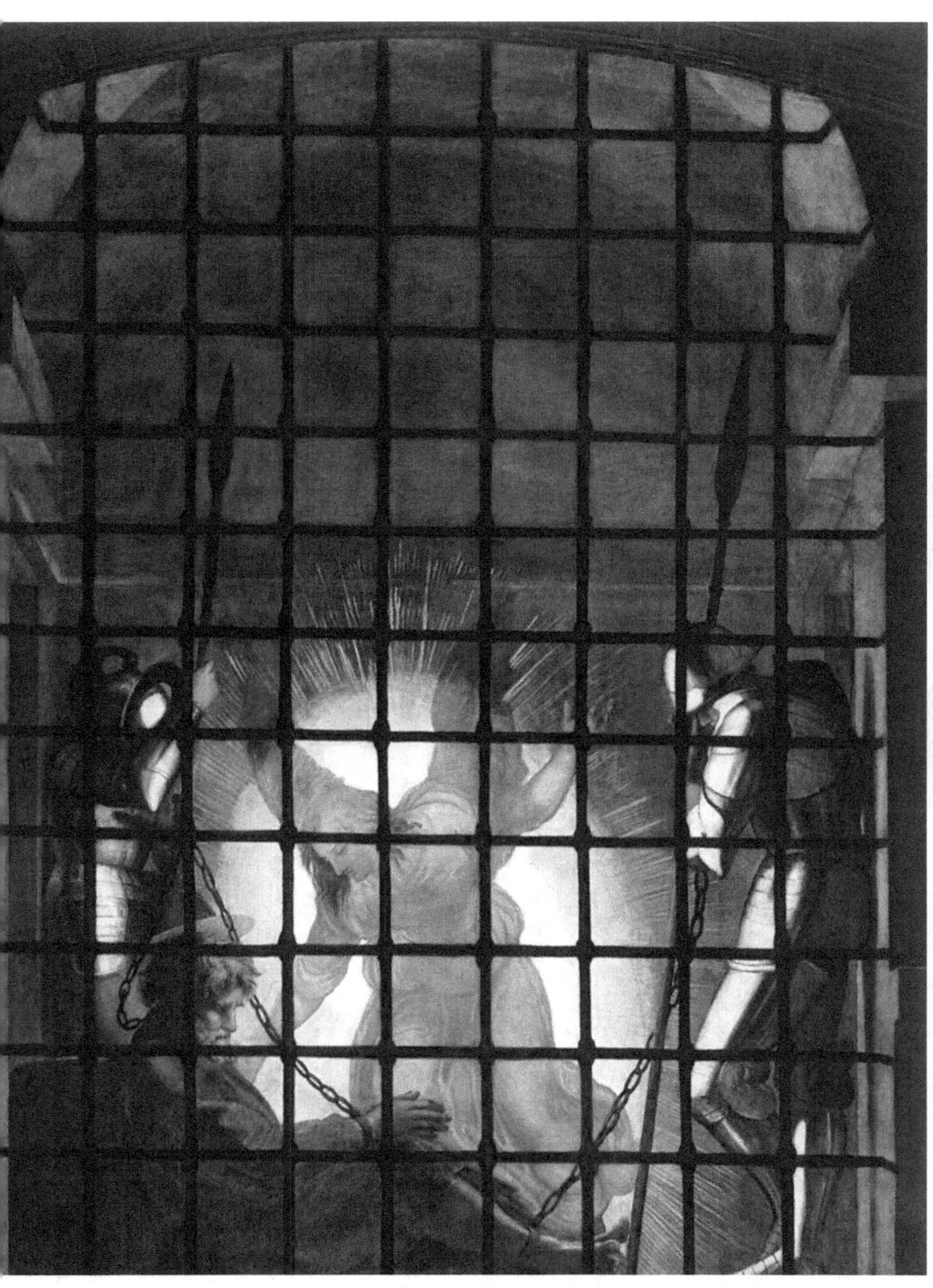

Raphael, The Liberation of St Peter

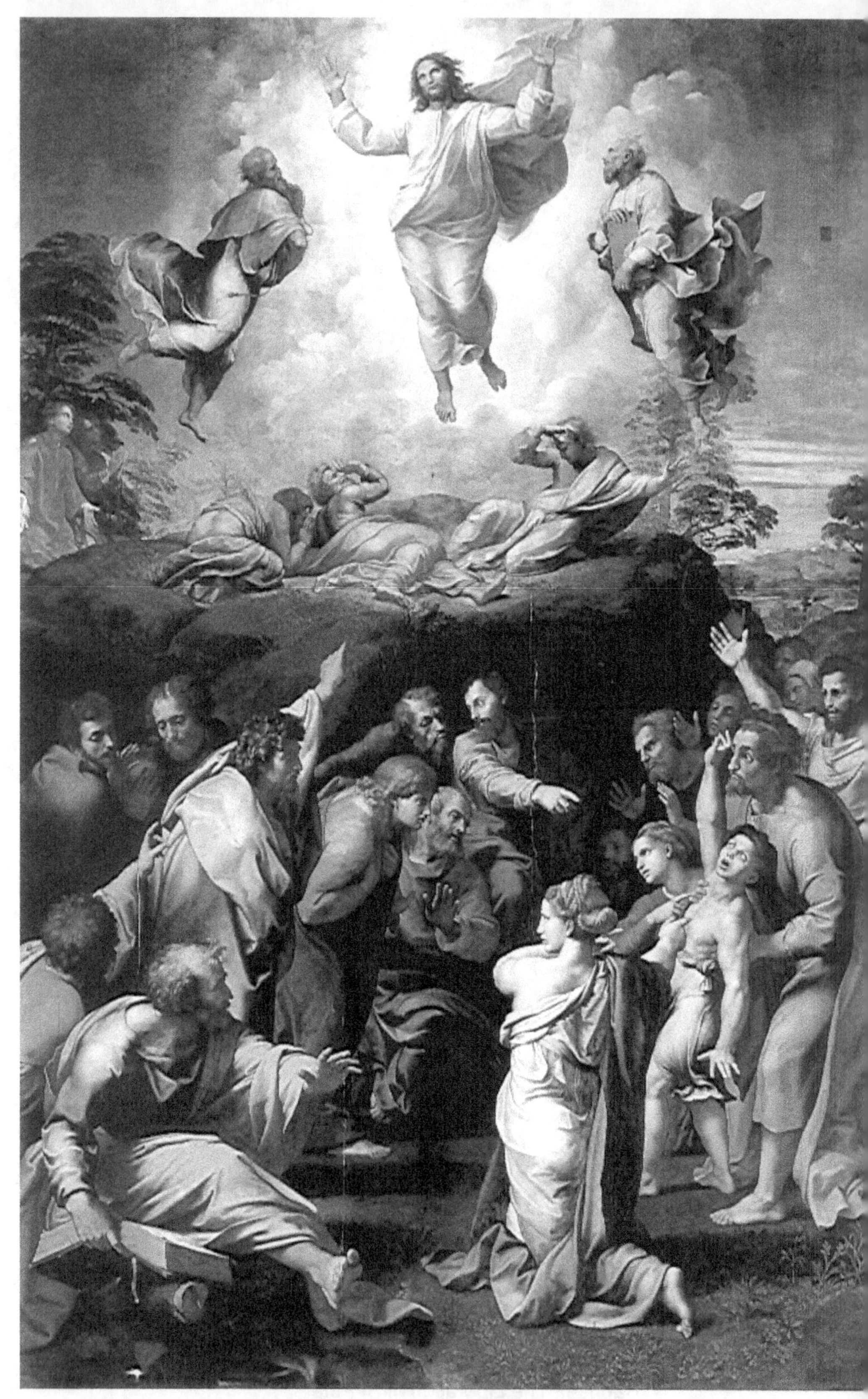

Raphael, Transfiguration, 1516-20, Vatican

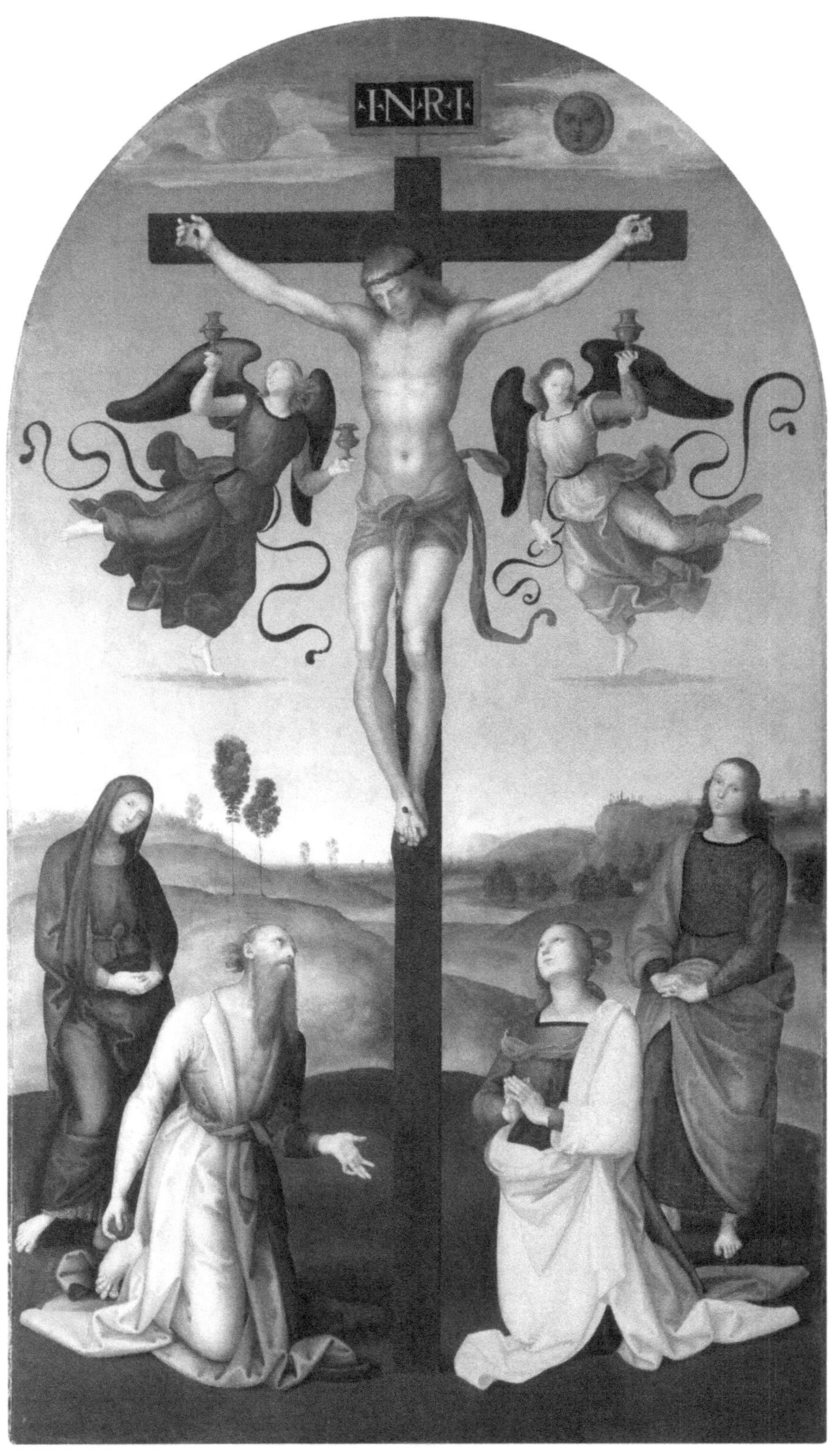

Raphael, The Mond Crucifion, 1502-03, National Gallery, London

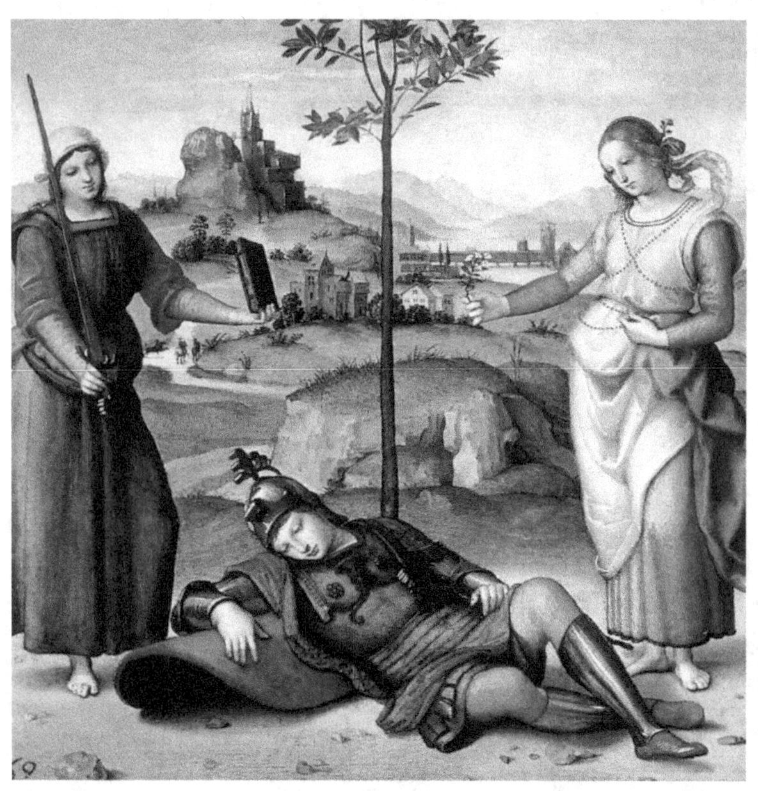

Raphael, Vision of a Knight, 1504,
National Gallery, London

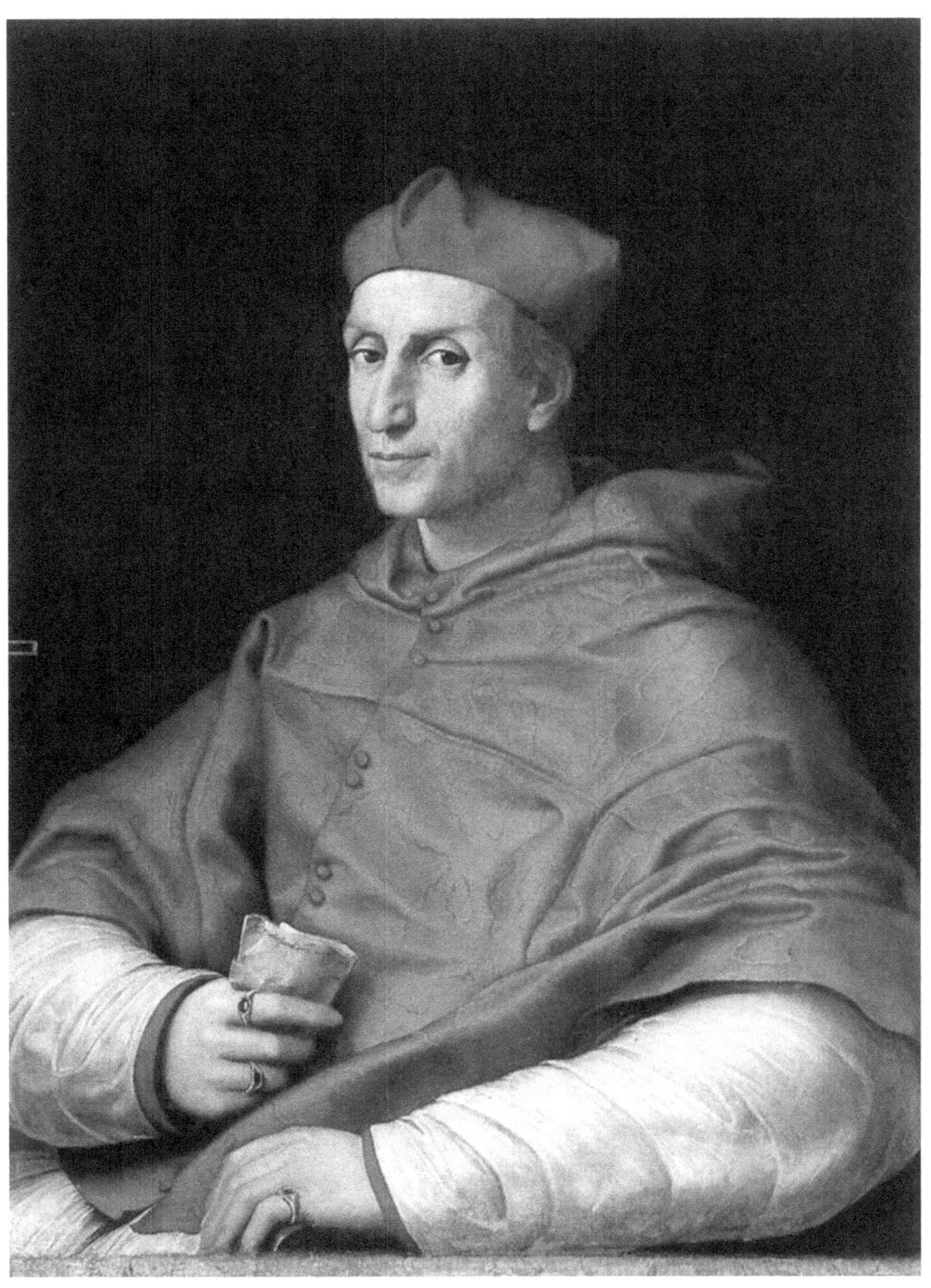

Raphael, Portrait of Cardinal Bibbiena, 1516, Pitti Palace

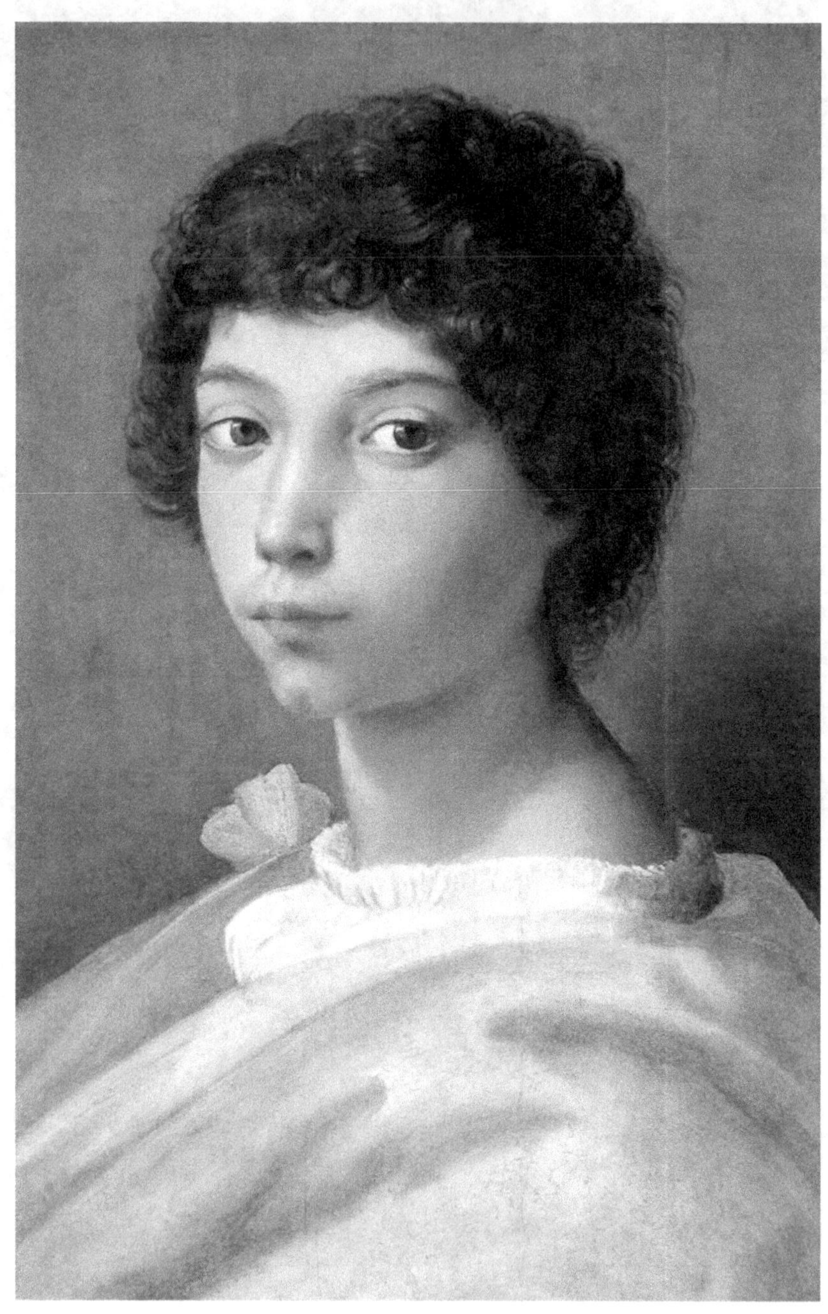

Raphael, Portrait of a Young Man, Madrid

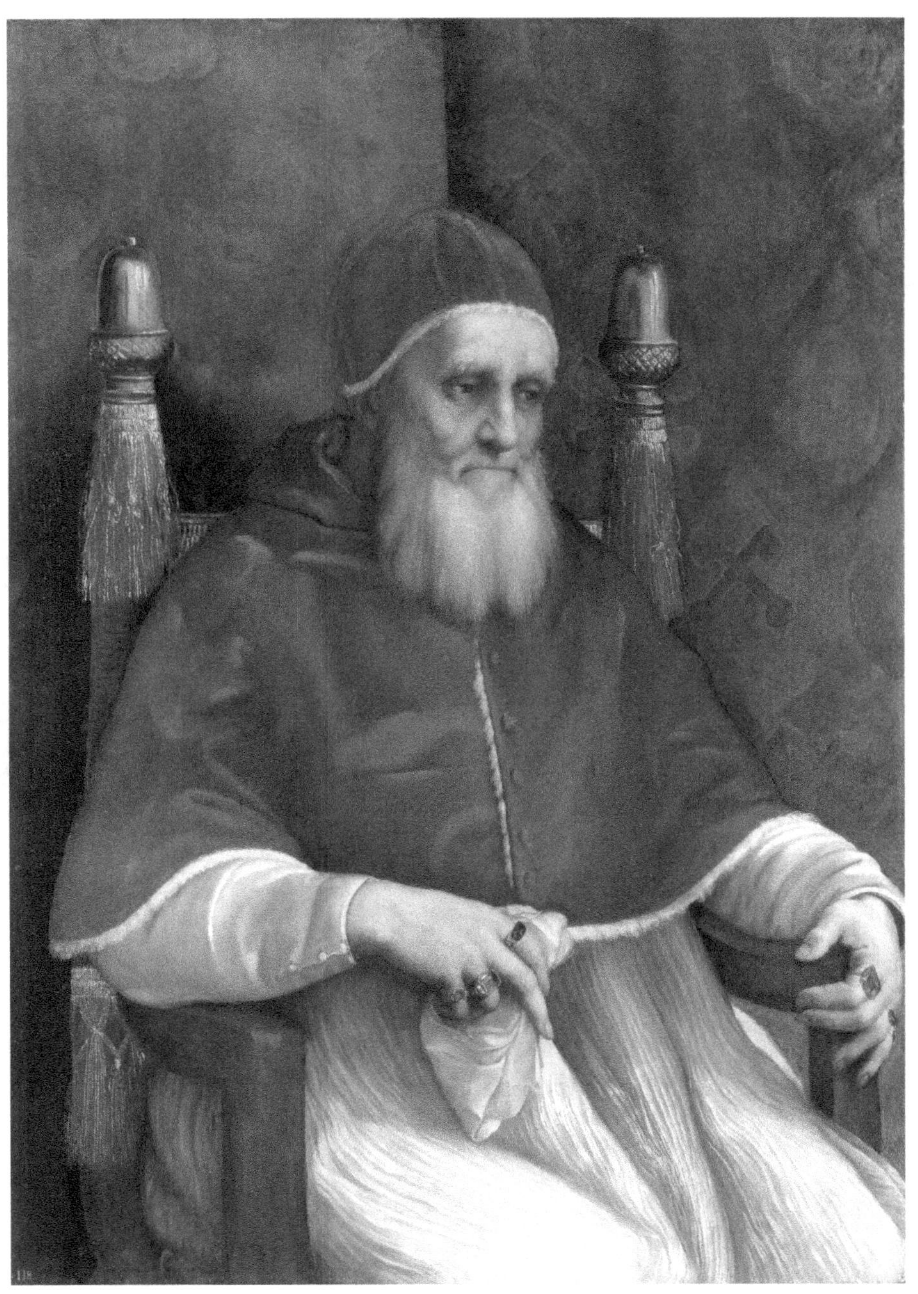

Raphael, Pope Julius II, 1512, Frankfurt

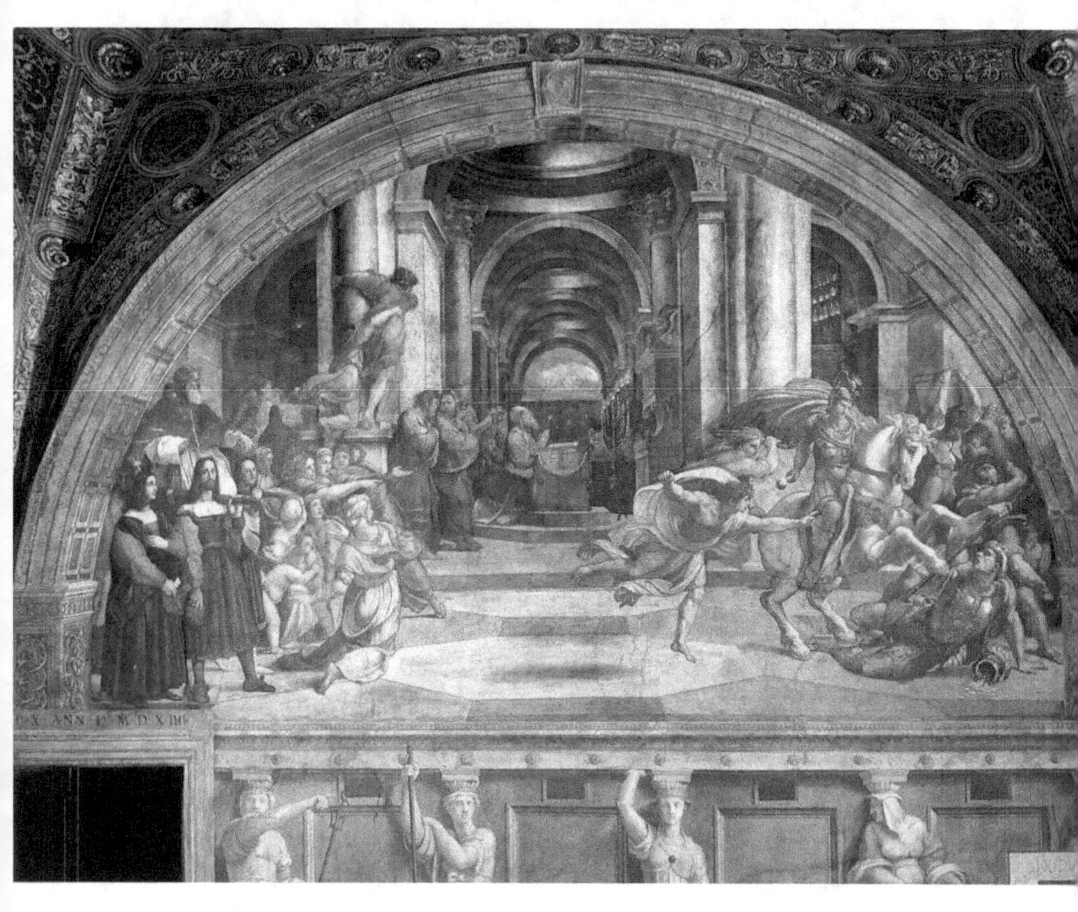

Raphael, Heliodorus Driven From the Temple, 1511-15

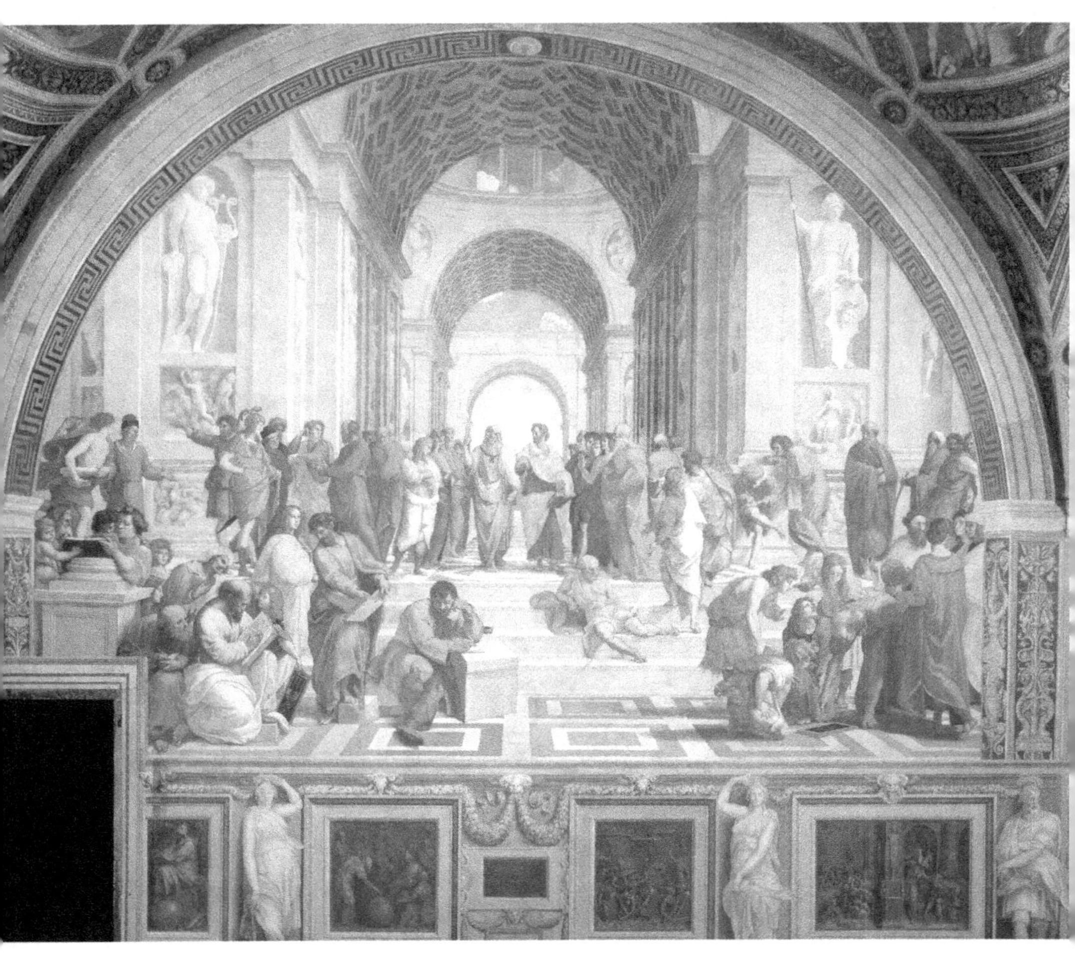

Raphael, School of Athens, 1511, Vatican

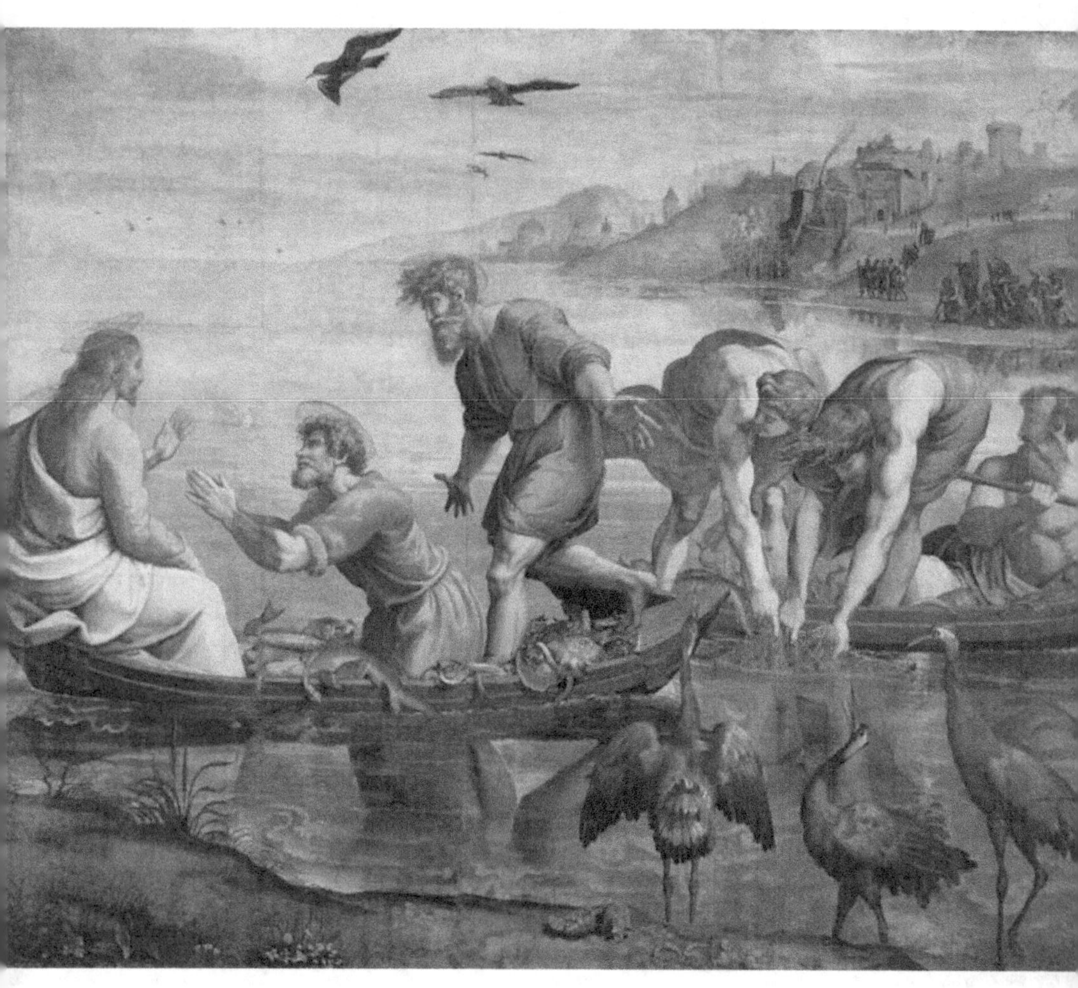

Raphael, The Raphael Cartoons, V & A Museum, London
(this page and over)

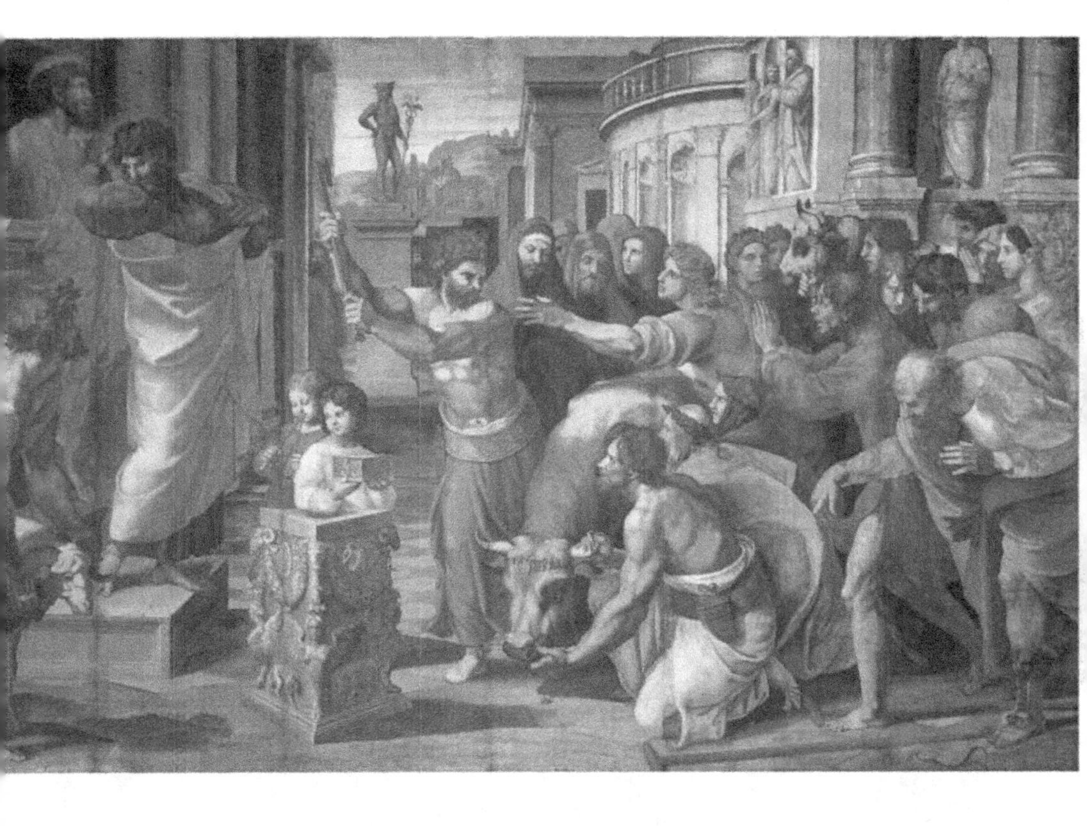

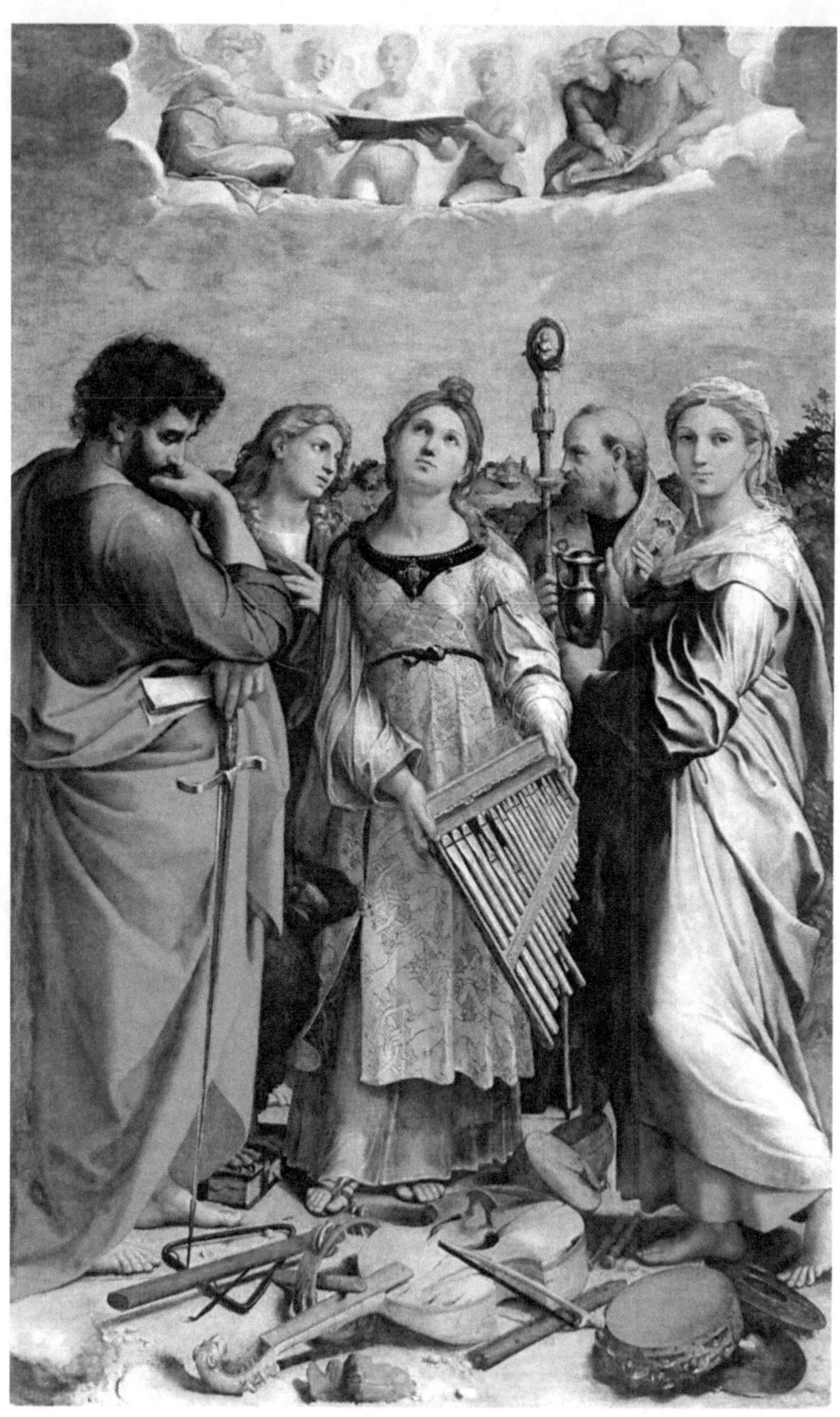

Raphael, St Cecilia

III

Raphael came to Rome before September 1508, for on the 5th of that month he sent a letter from the city of the popes to Francia at Bologna, whom he had probably met at Urbino. It must have been an intoxicating experience for the young master to find himself suddenly surrounded by the wonders of the classic world which at that time dominated the whole world of thought so that Christianity itself became permeated with Paganism; and to be as suddenly raised from the modest position, which in Florence had made him look with awe and veneration upon Michelangelo and Lionardo, to independent responsibility, as the compeer of the greatest of his calling. From the very first Pope Julius II. seems to have placed the utmost confidence in the newcomer, and the manner in which Raphael accomplished the first task set to him by his mighty patron not only justified this confidence but apparently made the Pope dissatisfied with much of the decorative work that had been executed in the Vatican rooms before the advent of the Urbinate.

Julius II.'s hatred of his predecessor, Alexander VI., had made it distasteful for him to live in the apartments that had been occupied by the Borgia Pope, so that he decided, in 1507, to move into the upper rooms of the Vatican, which, under the pontificate of Nicholas V., had been decorated by Pier dei Franceschi and Bramantino. These frescoes, however, did not find favour with the new Pope, who enlisted the services of Perugino, Peruzzi, Sodoma, Signorelli, and Pinturicchio for the redecoration of the *Stanze*, and finally entrusted Raphael with the painting of four medallions in Sodoma's ceiling in the first room, the Camera della Signatura. There has been some divergence of opinion as to the use of this room, but the subjects of the decorative scheme clearly point towards its being originally intended for a library. The allegorical figures of Theology, Philosophy, Jurisprudence, and Poetry with which Raphael filled the four medallions of the vaulted ceiling, were often used for the decoration of libraries during the late Renaissance; and the frequent occurrence of books in all the compositions lends further probability to this theory.

So delighted was Julius II. with the manner in which Raphael had acquitted himself of his first commission, that he, forthwith, charged him with the decoration of the entire suite of four rooms, and ruthlessly decreed the destruction of all the fresco-work previously done by other hands. But Raphael, in his hour of victory, gave proof of that generous and amiable disposition which endeared him to all with whom he came in contact. He prevailed upon his impetuous employer to save some of the work of Baldassare Peruzzi and of Perugino, and Sodoma's ceiling decoration in the Camera della Signatura. A series of heads by Bramantino, "so beautiful and so perfectly executed, that the power of speech alone was required to give them life," had to go, but before their destruction Raphael had them copied by one of his assistants. After his death these copies were presented by Giulio Romano to Paolo Giovio, and it is more than probable that they are identical with the "Bramantino" portraits from the Willett collection, now at the Metropolitan Museum, New York, and at South Kensington. Sir Caspar Pardon Clarke, the director of the former institution, at least favours this theory which I first advanced in the *New York Herald* in 1905.

•

But to return to Raphael's work in the Camera della Signatura, the thought and knowledge and learning displayed in the whole scheme either prove that the young master rapidly fell into line with the intellectual movement of his day, or that he wisely sought the advice of those who stood at the head of this movement. Indeed, we know of a letter in which he asks the poet Ariosto to advise him about certain details. Moreover, the Pope himself, no doubt, suggested his own ideas to his favourite painter; whilst the cultured Cardinal Bibbiena, Count Baldassare Castiglione, and the famous humanist Pietro Bembo, his intimate friends, were ever at his disposal, and Bramante probably assisted him in designing the architectural setting to his groups. Raphael himself, though extraordinarily receptive, and better able than anybody else to clothe an idea in the most perfect pictorial forms, was not a man of learning. With Dante's and Petrarch's poetry he must have been made familiar in his father's house. He had probably dipped into the writings of Marsilio Ficino, and also acquired a knowledge of the rudiments of classic lore; but that he never mastered the Latin tongue, which was then a *sine quâ non* of all real culture and learning, is clearly evident from the fact that in the closing years of his life, when he held the appointment of inspector of antiquities, he had to enlist the learned humanist Andrea Fulvio to translate for him the Latin inscriptions on classic ruins.

In the Camera della Signatura, Raphael's entire decoration has the same sense of orderly arrangement, the same unity of conception in the endless variety of *motif* and incident, as each individual fresco of the scheme. On the pendentives, which connect the ceiling medallions with the large frescoes on the walls, he painted the "Fall of Man" next to "Theology," the "Judgment of Solomon" next to "Law," the "Triumph of Apollo over Marsyas" to accompany "Poetry," and an allegorical represent-ation of "Astronomy" (or "Natural Science") to go with "Philosophy." After an enormous amount of preparatory work he proceeded to fill the large wall under "Theology" with the wonderful monumental fresco known as the "Disputa del Sacramento," which, far from representing a dispute, shows the confessors and saints and fathers of the Church (and among them Dante, Savonarola, and Fra Angelico) united in acknowledging the triumph of the Church and the miracle of the Eucharist.

On the opposite wall, under "Philosophy," is the so-called "School of Athens," in which, in accordance with the contradictory spirit of the age, the philosophic systems of the ancient world are glorified in the same manner as is Christianity in the "Disputa." In that nobly-arranged group of philosophers, Raphael's friends and contemporaries – Bramante, Lionardo, Castiglione, Francesco della Rovere, Federigo Gonzaga, Sodoma, the artist himself, and many others – figure in the guise of Euclid, Plato, Zoroaster, and other sages. Raphael's compositional skill was not baffled by the awkward intrusion of large door-frames into the space of the remaining two walls, on one of which, under the Poetry medallion, he depicted "Parnassus," with the muses and poets (Homer, Virgil, Dante, Ariosto, Boccaccio, Tebaldeo, Sappho, &c.) grouped around Apollo, who plays a viol instead of the customary lyre. Above the door on the last wall are allegorical figures of Fortitude, Prudence, and Temperance, and at the sides "Justinian delivering the Pandects," and "Gregory IX." (impersonated by Julius II.) promulgating the Decretals. The entire room was finished before November 1511.

It was probably in the same year that Raphael painted the magnificent portrait of Julius II. at the Pitti Palace, stern of feature and careworn, as he well might have appeared at this time of political disaster culminating in the loss of Bologna. But when Raphael set about the decoration of the "Stanza of Heliodorus," the Pope's star was again in the ascendant, and his policy had achieved the signal triumph of defeating the French and driving them out of the country. The subjects chosen for the decoration of this room are in consequence more or less directly connected with these events, especially the fresco from which the apartment derives its name: the "Expulsion of Heliodorus from the Temple of Jerusalem" – an obvious allusion to the expulsion of the French forces. The fresco is remarkable for the effective contrast of the tumultuous dramatic movement on the right, and the stately repose of the group on the left, around the majestically enthroned figure of Pope Julius II.

The same potentate of the Church appears kneeling opposite the officiating priest in the fresco of the "Mass of Bolsena," which illustrates the miracle of drops of blood appearing from the Host before the eyes of the priest who doubts the dogma of the transubstantiation, an event which has led to the institution of the Corpus Christi celebration. The fresco was probably inspired by Julius himself, who had visited the chapel of Bolsena on his campaign against Bologna, and perhaps made a vow on this occasion to commemorate his visit by a votive offering. This "Mass of Bolsena" fresco is remarkable for the almost Venetian glow of warm colour, a result, no doubt, of the knowledge imparted to Raphael by Sebastiano del Piombo, who had come to Rome from Venice in 1511. The wall opposite illustrates the "Liberation of St. Peter from Prison," which is, however, not an allusion, as has been suggested, to Leo X.'s escape from French captivity, since it was begun under the régime of Julius II., who more probably intended it to signify the Deliverance of the Church. On the last wall is depicted the "Retreat of Attila before St. Leo," with Leo X., who had succeeded Julius II. in 1513, impersonating his namesake, but there is little of Raphael's handiwork in this fresco, the execution of which is almost entirely due to his assistants. The decoration of this stanza was completed in 1514, a year which brought further honours and duties to Raphael who was then appointed to succeed Bramante as architect of St. Peter's.

Henceforth Raphael is to be considered rather as the head of a little army of painters and craftsmen, whom he supplied with ideas and designs to be executed under his directions, than as a master who is to be held responsible for the working out of every detail in the works which were turned out from his bottega with his sanction, and under his name. Even in the early years of his Roman period, comparatively few of the altar-pieces and easel pictures commissioned from him were entirely the work of his brush. In the ever popular "Madonna della Sedia," at the Pitti Palace, we have pure Raphael, and also in the masterpiece known as the "Madonna di Foligno," which was painted for the Pope's Chamberlain Sigismondi dei Conti, for his family chapel in the church of Ara Coeli in 1512, in commemoration of this dignitary's escape from a bursting fireball, as is indicated by the meteor in the landscape background. This picture was subsequently removed to Sigismondo's birthplace Foligno, whence it was carried off by the French in 1797, but had to be eventually restored, and is now among the treasures of the Vatican. The sadly deteriorated "Madonna of the Tower," at the National Gallery, and the "Madonna di Casa d'Alba," at the Hermitage, are probably of the master's own execution; but Giulio Romano and other pupils must be held responsible for the "Vierge au Diadème," the "Madonna del divino Amore," the "Garvagh Madonna," the "Madonna of the Fish," the "Madonna of the Candelabra," and several other well-known pictures for which Raphael had supplied the designs.

IV

A letter written by Raphael to his uncle Simone Ciarla on the 1st of July 1514 is of incalculable importance for the light it throws upon the master's private life and character. It is written by a man flushed with success, but modest withal – in the full enjoyment of all the gifts that fortune and his talent and tact have brought to him, but in no way overbearing or boastful. And through it all sounds a note of cool calculation – in money matters as well as in the weighing of matrimonial chances. He states the amount of his fortune, of his salary as architect of St. Peter's, and of the payments that are to be made to him for "work in hand." And in the same way he refers to an "advantageous match" proposed to him by Cardinal Bibbiani, to which he has already pledged himself, but should it fall to the ground, "I will fall in with your wishes" – a reference apparently to an eligible matrimonial candidate in Urbino. Nor are there chances lacking in Rome, where, indeed, he knows of a pretty girl with a dowry of 3000 gold crowns! He also mentions with no little pride that he is living in Rome in his own house.

These remarks about his matrimonial schemes take us to one of the most interesting and most disputed chapters of Raphael's life – his irregular attachment to the "Bella Fornarina," the beautiful daughter of a baker from Siena, which is referred to first by Vasari, and then, in 1665, by Fabio Chigi, and has been treated as mere invention by many modern writers. The evidence collected by Signor Rodolfo Lanciani proves, however, the truth of Vasari's story, and furthermore establishes the name and ultimate fate of the "Fornarina." According to local tradition, three houses in Rome are pointed out as the successive homes of Raphael's *inamorata*; and each of these houses is in close proximity to the buildings, on the decoration of which the master was successively employed. The first of these houses in the Via di Sta. Dorotea is still occupied by a bakery known as "il forno della Fornarina;" the second is in the Vicolo del Cedro near St. Egidio in Trastevere; and the third is the Palazzetto Sassi, which has a tablet let into the wall with an inscription to the effect that "Tradition says that the one who became so dear to Raphael, and whom he raised to fame, lived in this house."

It has now been ascertained from a census return made under Leo X. in 1518, that one of the houses of the Sassi family was occupied by the baker Francesco from Siena, which completely tallies with the tradition that "Margherita, donna di Raffaello," as she is described in a contemporary marginal note in a copy of the Giunta edition of Vasari in 1568, was the daughter of a baker from Siena. But even more decisive is the proof which was found in 1897 in an entry in the ledger of the Congregation of Sant'Apollonia in Trastevere, a kind of home for fallen and repentant women. This entry, which is under the date of the 18th August 1520, that is a little over four months after Raphael's death, runs as follows: "A di 18 Augusti 1520 Hoggi e stata recenta nel nro Conservatorio maa Margarita vedoa, figliola del quondam Francescho Luti da Siena." ("August 18, 1520. – To-day has been received into our establishment the widow *Margarita, daughter of the late Francesco Luti of Siena.*") The remarkable coincidence of dates and names leaves no doubt that this "widow" was the Bella Fornarina, Margherita, the daughter of the baker Francesco from Siena, and the beautiful creature who served Raphael as model for the "Donna Velata," for the "Sistine Madonna," and for one of the heads in the "St. Cecilia."

The story goes that Raphael's attachment lasted up to the time of his death, when, on the insistence of the Pope's messenger who was to bring the dying man the benediction, she was removed from the room. Vasari also relates that in his will Raphael "left her a sufficient provision wherewith she might live in decency." His long infatuation with the baker's daughter may well account for his unwillingness to enter into the bonds of matrimony even with as desirable and noble a partner as Cardinal Bernardo Divizio's niece, Maria Bibbiena, to whom he was practically engaged in 1514, and who after years of postponement is said to have died of a broken heart. Vasari's statement that Raphael's hesitation was due to the prospect of a cardinal's hat being bestowed upon him is utterly untrustworthy and contrary to all precedent and reason. It is much more likely that Raphael considered it diplomatic to humour a man in as powerful a position as Cardinal Bibbiena, and to agree to become engaged to his niece, even though his own position at the time was such that he could speak on terms of equality to cardinals, as may be gathered from this witty repartee recorded by his friend Baldassare Castiglione: Two cardinals, who examined a painting upon which he was just engaged, found fault with the redness of the complexion of St. Peter and St. Paul. "My Lords," retorted Raphael, "be not concerned; because I painted them so with full intention, since we have reason to believe that St. Peter and St. Paul are as red in Heaven as you see them here, for shame that their Church should be governed by such as you!"

But we must return to Raphael's work in the last decade of his life. He could now no longer devote himself entirely to the art of his choice, and found it utterly impossible to cope with the multitude of commissions that were showered upon him by the mighty of this earth, even though a swarm of assistants were constantly kept at work. The vain appeals of Isabella d'Este for a small painting from his hand prove the difficulty of obtaining such a favour. For Raphael was now the Pope's architect and superintendent of ceremonies, and in 1515 he was appointed inspector of antiquities in succession to Fra Giocondo of Verona.

He had to paint scenery and to design medals and plans; and on one occasion he was actually called upon to paint a life-size elephant on the walls of the Vatican!

Yet, with all these absorbing occupations he found time to model several reliefs for the Chigi tomb in the Chigi Chapel of St. Maria del Popolo, notably a panel of classic design representing "Christ and the Woman of Samaria," which was cast in bronze by Lorenzotto, who also executed in marble a statue of Jonah from a model by Raphael. He furnished the architectural designs of the Villa Madama for Giulio dei Medici (afterwards Clement VII.) and several other palaces in Rome, and also for the dainty Palazzo Pandolfini in Florence, where the alternating arched and triangular pediments are for the first time introduced in secular Renaissance architecture. He furnished the engraver Marcantonio Raimondi of Bologna with designs like the famous "Judgment of Paris." He planned and began an elaborate Cosmography of Rome; and yet in the midst of all his varied labours he found leisure to scribble some ardent love sonnets on his sheets of drawings. An example of his poetic effusions is preserved at the British Museum, and its ardent tone lends colour to Vasari's assertion that Raphael was extremely susceptible to the charms of the fair sex. The palace in which he lived in princely state was built by Bramante and bought by Raphael on October 7, 1517. In very much altered form it still stands in the Piazza di Scossacavalli at the corner of the Via di Borgo Nuovo. Since the present building has been identified as Raphael's palace, his studio has been discovered, cut into two apartments, but with a beautiful wooden ceiling by Bramante left intact.

In this studio he must have painted the greatest and most deservedly popular of his altar-pieces, the "Madonna di San Sisto," and the "Transfiguration," now at the Vatican Gallery, which was on his easel when death stayed his hand. Here, too, he probably painted that masterly portrait of "Baldassare Castiglione," which is one of the priceless treasures of the Louvre, and perhaps the magnificent group of "Leo X. with Cardinals

Giulio dei Medici and L. dei Rossi," now at the Pitti Palace. All the most notable men who were in Rome at that period passed through Raphael's studio, but of the portraits which he is known to have painted in Rome, comparatively few have come down to us. That of the humanist Tommaso Inghirami was until recently at the Inghirami Palace in Volterra, but has now gone across the Atlantic; one of Cardinal Bibbiena is in Madrid; and one of the Venetian humanists Navagero and Beazzano in the Doria Palace in Rome. Among the lost portraits are those of Pietro Bembo, of Giuliano dei Medici, Duke of Nemours, of Federigo Gonzaga, and of Lorenzo, Duke of Urbino.

Meanwhile Raphael's pupils had been busy with the decoration of the remaining two *Stanze* of the Vatican after Raphael's designs. In the Stanza dell'Incendio del Borgo, which was decorated for Leo. X. between 1514–1517, Giulio Romano had painted the "Battle of Ostia" and most of the "Incendio del Borgo," though parts of the latter, which illustrates the staying of the great conflagration by Leo IV.'s prayer, are unquestionably Raphael's own. The last room, called the Hall of Constantine, was almost entirely painted after the master's death by his pupils, who also had the chief share in the execution of the fifty-two scriptural subjects in the Loggia of the Vatican, which are known as "The Bible of Raphael." Most of this work was done by Perino del Vaga, while Giovanni da Udine added the arabesques and grotesques round the panels. But all this has suffered much from exposure to the elements, and has been entirely repainted.

For Agostino Chigi's Villa Farnesina, Raphael painted the beautiful "Galatea" fresco, which may be considered the supreme expression of the spirit of the Renaissance. This merchant prince gave the master another opportunity for displaying his decorative skill, when he employed him in adorning the Chigi Chapel in St. Maria della Pace. The Sibyls and Angels of these frescoes afford the most striking instance of Michelangelo's influence upon Raphael; and it is a curious coincidence that it was just in reference to this work that Michelangelo was called upon to express his opinion as to the fairness of Raphael's charge of 500 ducats. That small jealousy was not one of Buonarroti's faults appears from the generous valuation of 900 ducats he put upon his rival's work.

In 1515–1516 Raphael designed the cartoons for the tapestries which were to complete the decoration of the Sistine Chapel. The cartoons were translated into the material by the looms of Flanders at a cost of 34,000 scudi; and these tapestries are now, after many wanderings, and after having suffered much dilapidation, housed on the upper floor of the Vatican. Seven of the cartoons, cut into strips for the exigencies of the loom, were discovered in Flanders by Rubens, and purchased on his advice by Charles I. in 1630. On the breaking up of the ill-fated king's collection, they were saved from transportation by Oliver Cromwell and are now at the Victoria and Albert Museum. The execution of these cartoons is almost entirely due to Gian Francesco Penni, and the borders of the tapestries were designed by Giovanni da Usline. About 1516 Raphael also decorated Cardinal Bibbiena's bathroom with the "Triumphs of Venus and Cupid," in Pompeian style. The frescoes are still in existence, but are not accessible to the public.

In the early days of April 1520 Raphael was attacked by a fever which he had probably contracted in superintending some excavations. He made his last will on the 4th of April and died on the 6th. That he repented of his treatment of Maria Bibbiena is fairly evident from the epitaph which, by his wish, was placed upon her tomb: "We, Baldassare Turini da Pescia and Gianbattista Branconi dall'Aquila, testamentary executors and recipients of the last wishes of Raphael, have raised this memorial to his affianced wife, Maria, daughter of Antonio da Bibbiena, whom death deprived of a happy marriage." After providing for the Fornarina, so that she might "live in decency," he left his fortune of 16,000 ducats to his relatives, and his drawings and sketches to his favourite pupils Giulio Romano and Penni. He was buried in the Pantheon in close proximity to Maria Bibbiena. His epitaph

was written by Cardinal Bembo, and Count Baldassare Castiglione also put his grief into the shape of a beautiful sonnet.

"The death of Raphael," says Vasari, "was bitterly deplored
by all the Papal court, not only because he had formed part
thereof, since he had held the office of chamberlain to the Pontiff,
but also because Leo X. had esteemed him so highly, that his loss
occasioned that sovereign the bitterest grief. Oh, most happy and
thrice blessed spirit, of whom all are proud to speak, whose
actions are celebrated with praise by all men, and the least of
whose works left behind thee is admired and prized."

Illustrations on the following pages are from some of the contemporaries of Raphael.

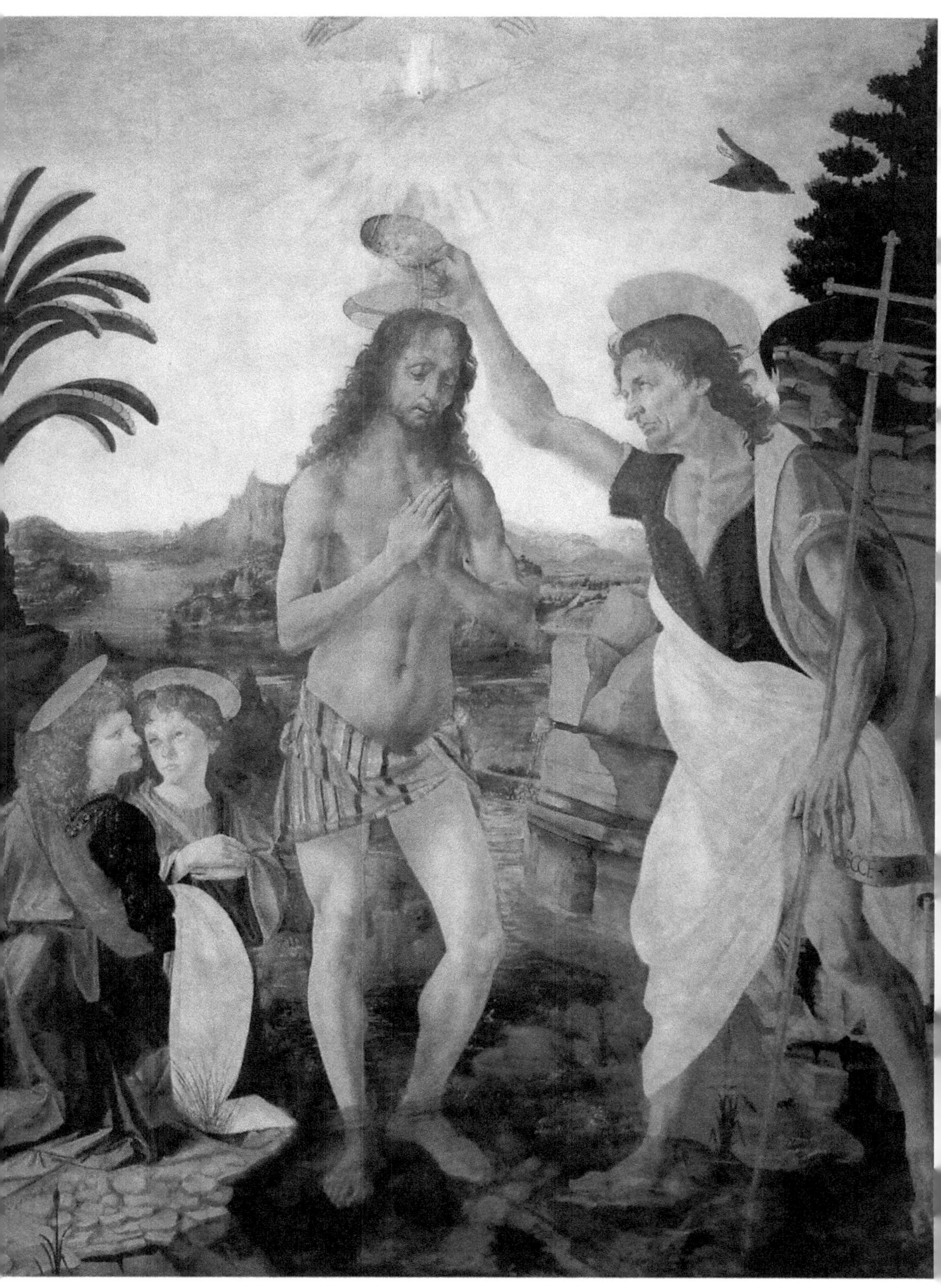

Andrea del Verrocchio, The Baptism of Christ

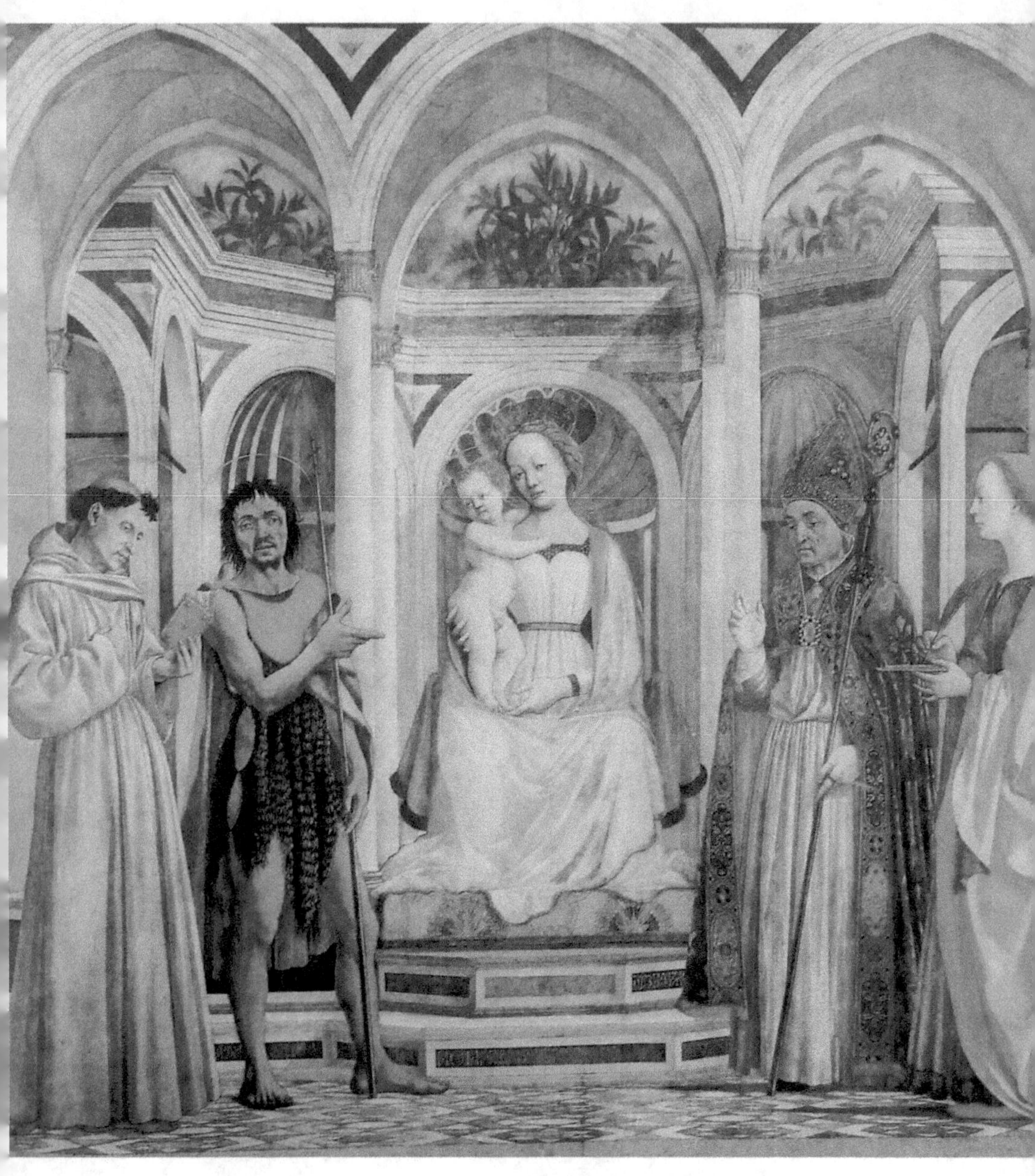

Domenico Veneziano, Madonna and Child With Saints, 1445, Uffizi Gallery

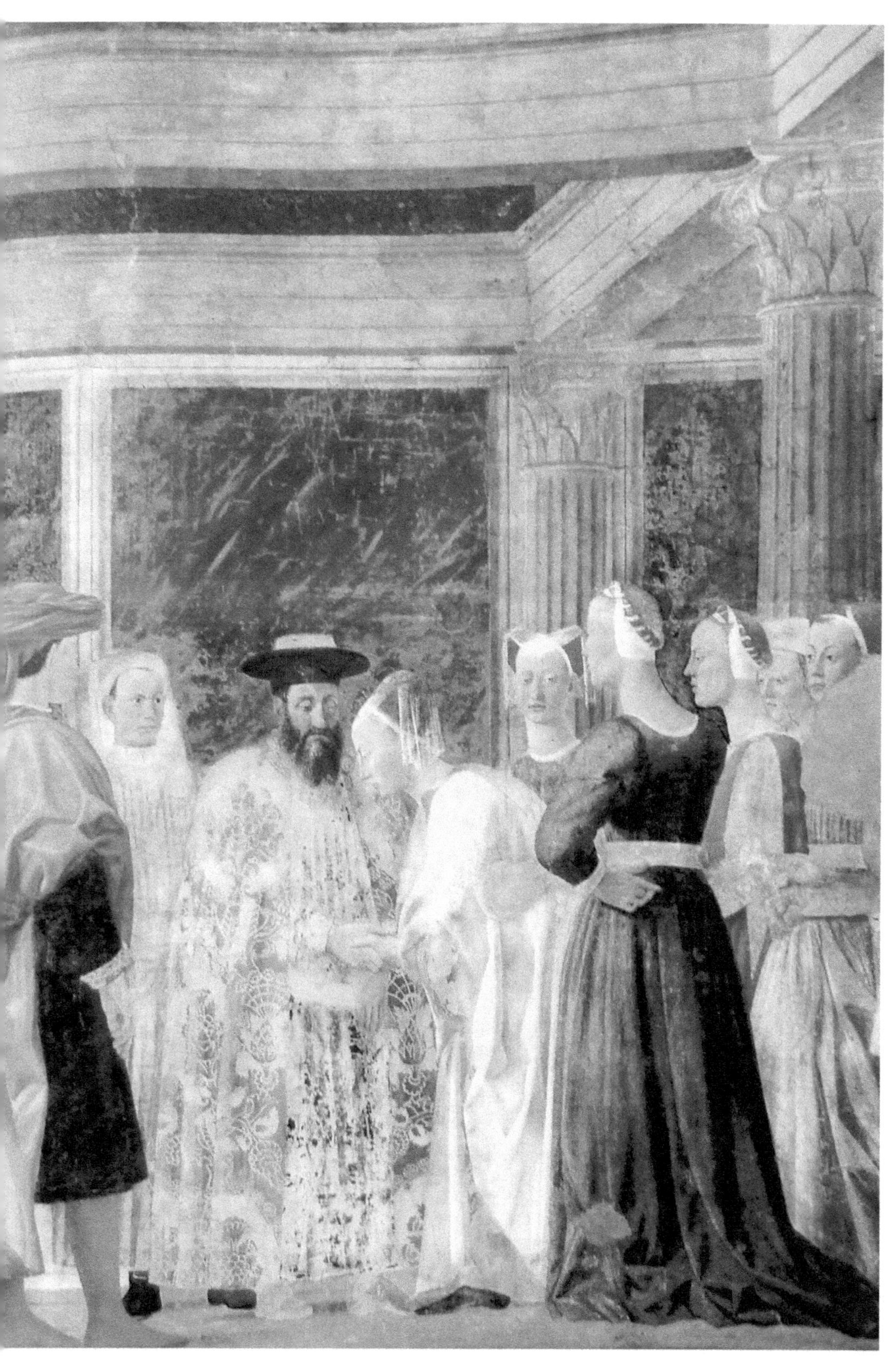

Piero della Francesca, frescoes, Arezzo

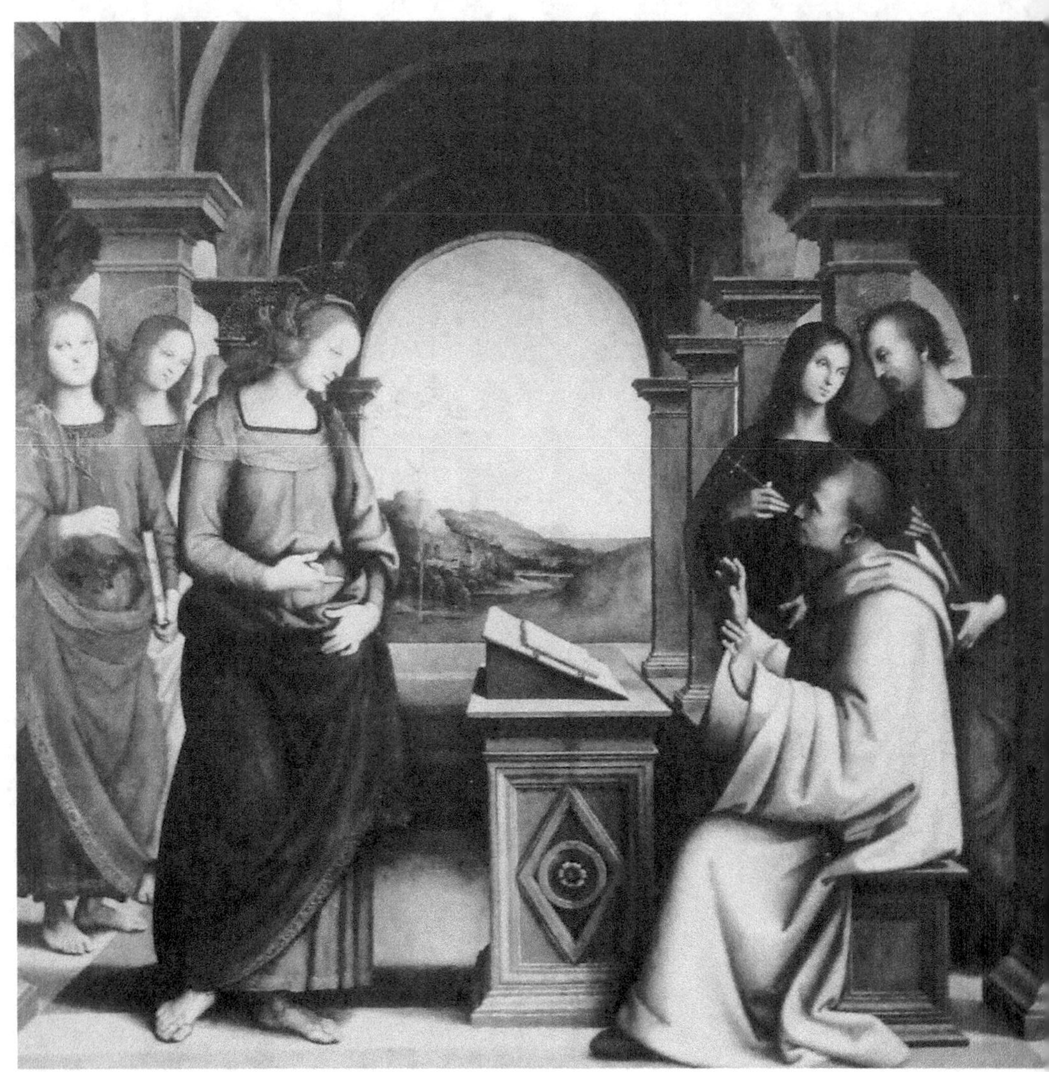

Perugino, Vision of St Bernard, 1488

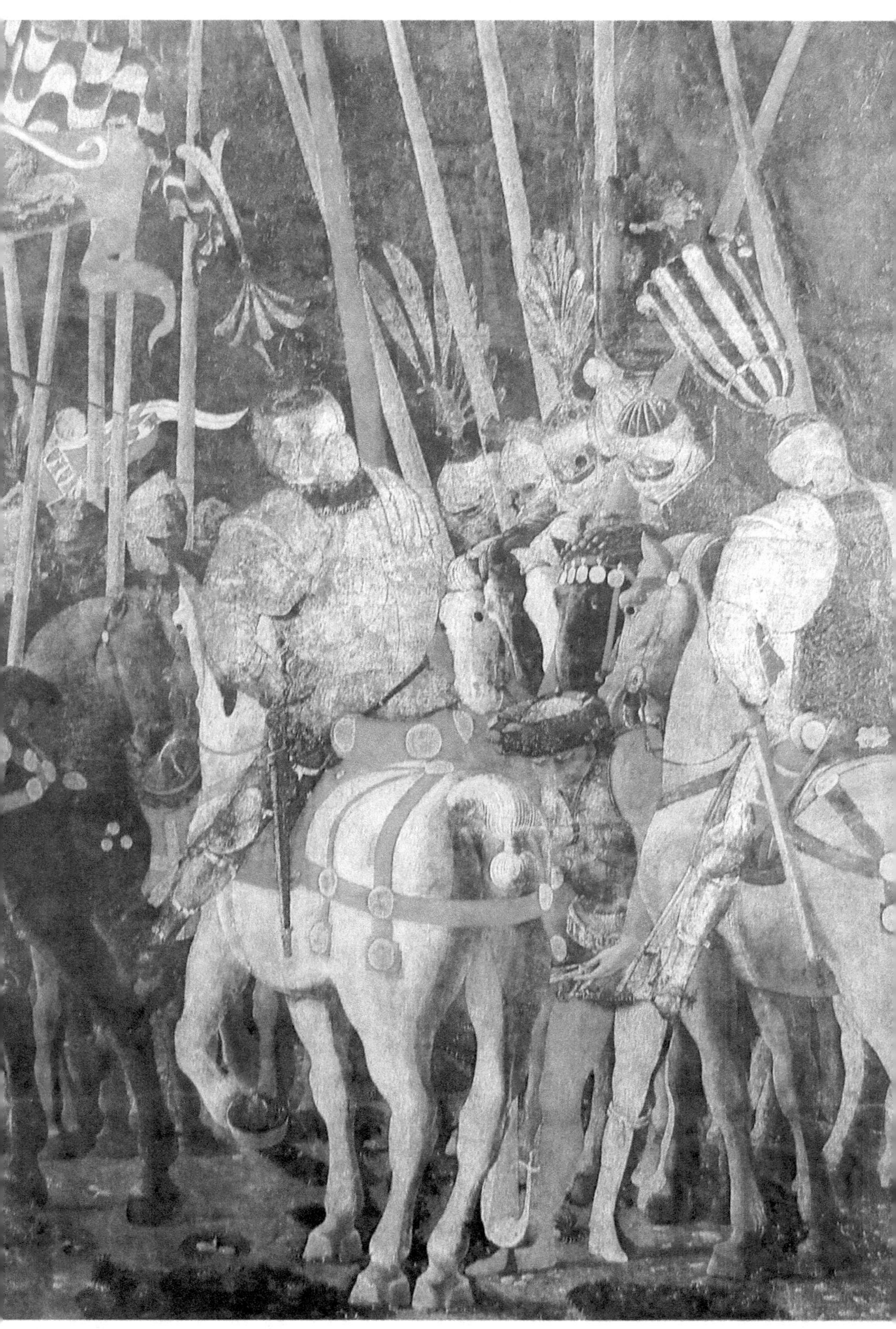

Paolo Uccello, The Battle of San Romano, Paris

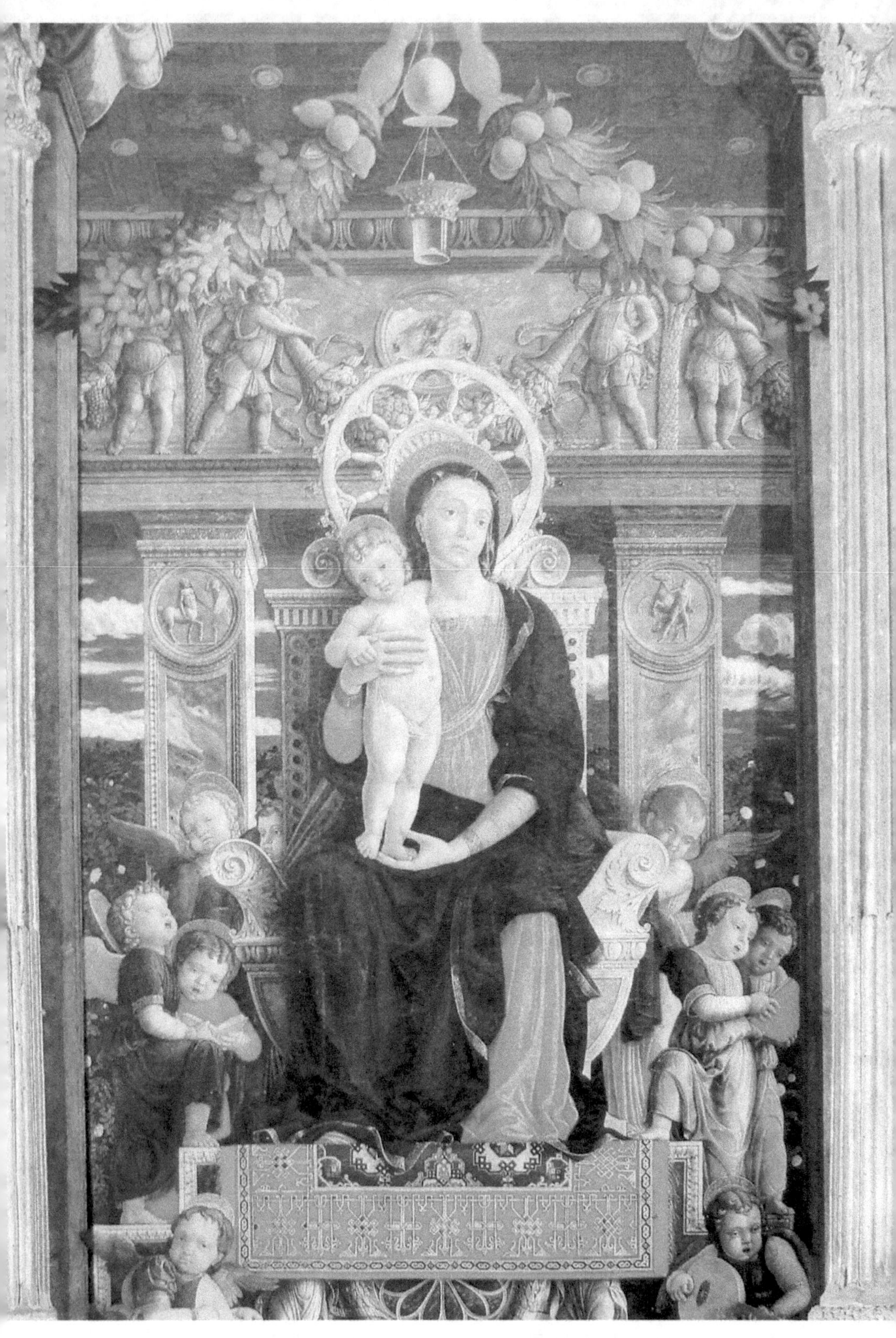

Andreas Mantegna, Madonna and Child Enthroned, 1457-60, Verona

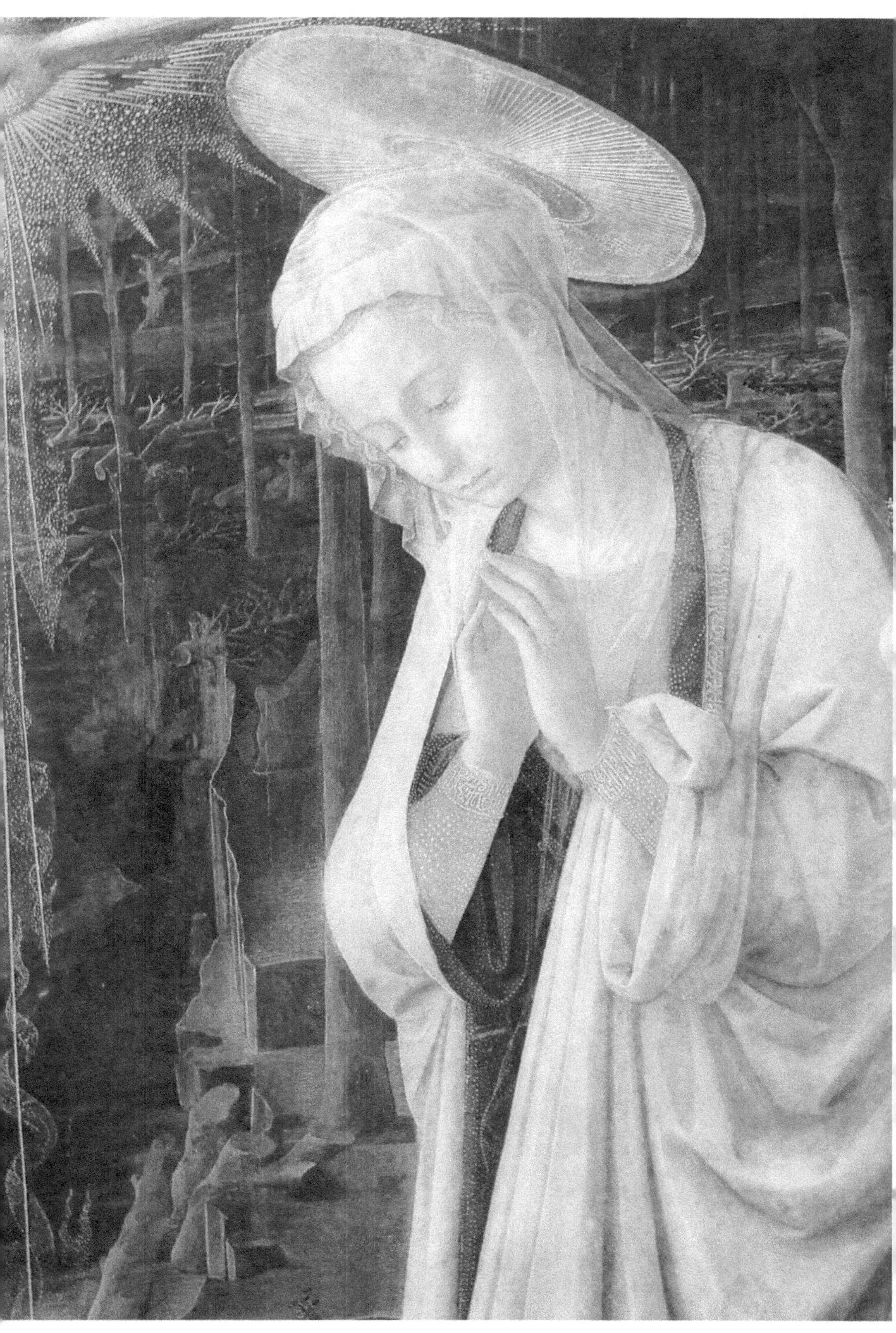

Fra Filippo Lippi, The Adoration of the Virgin, Berlin, detail

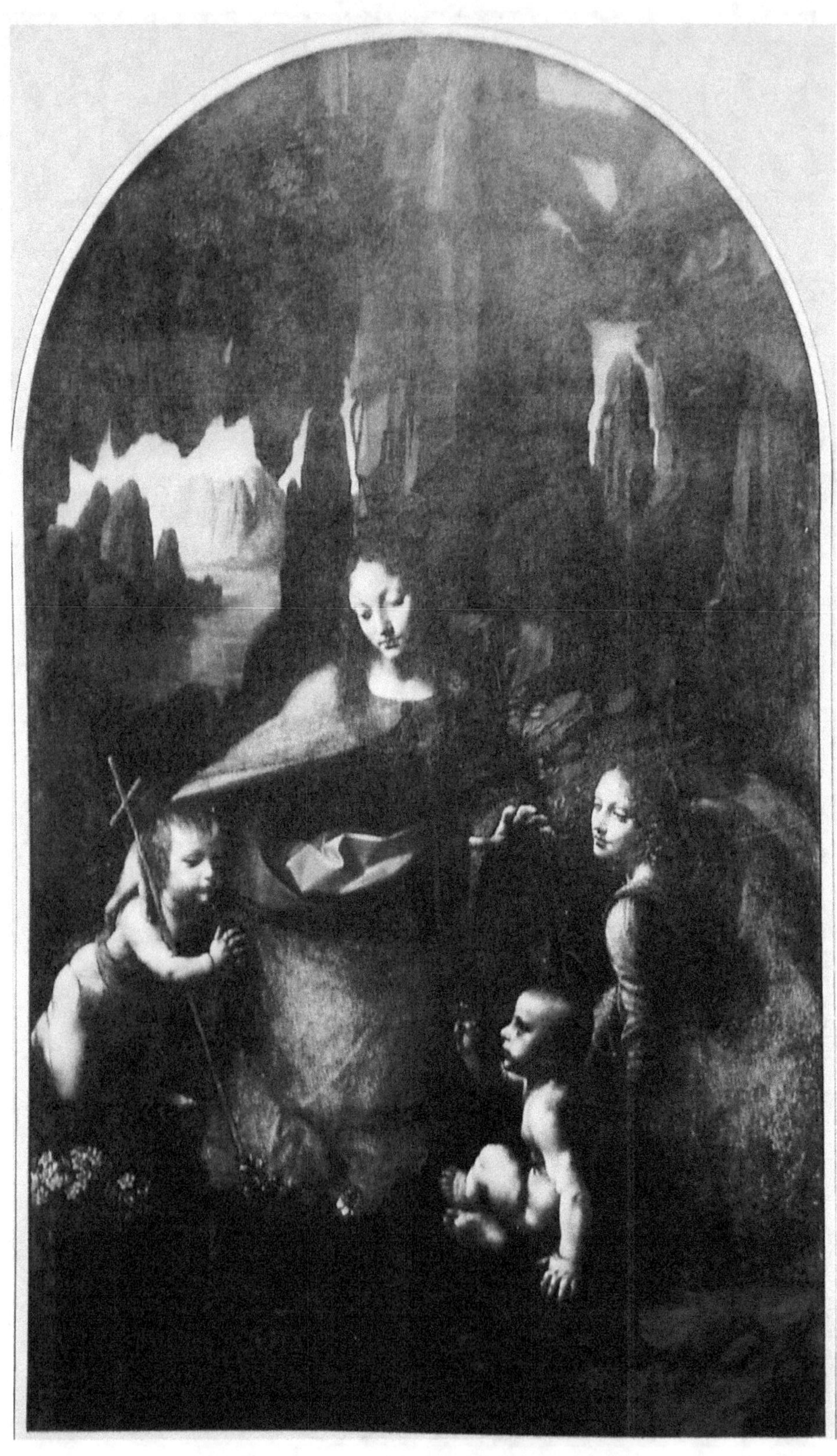

Leonardo da Vinci, The Madonna of the Rocks, London

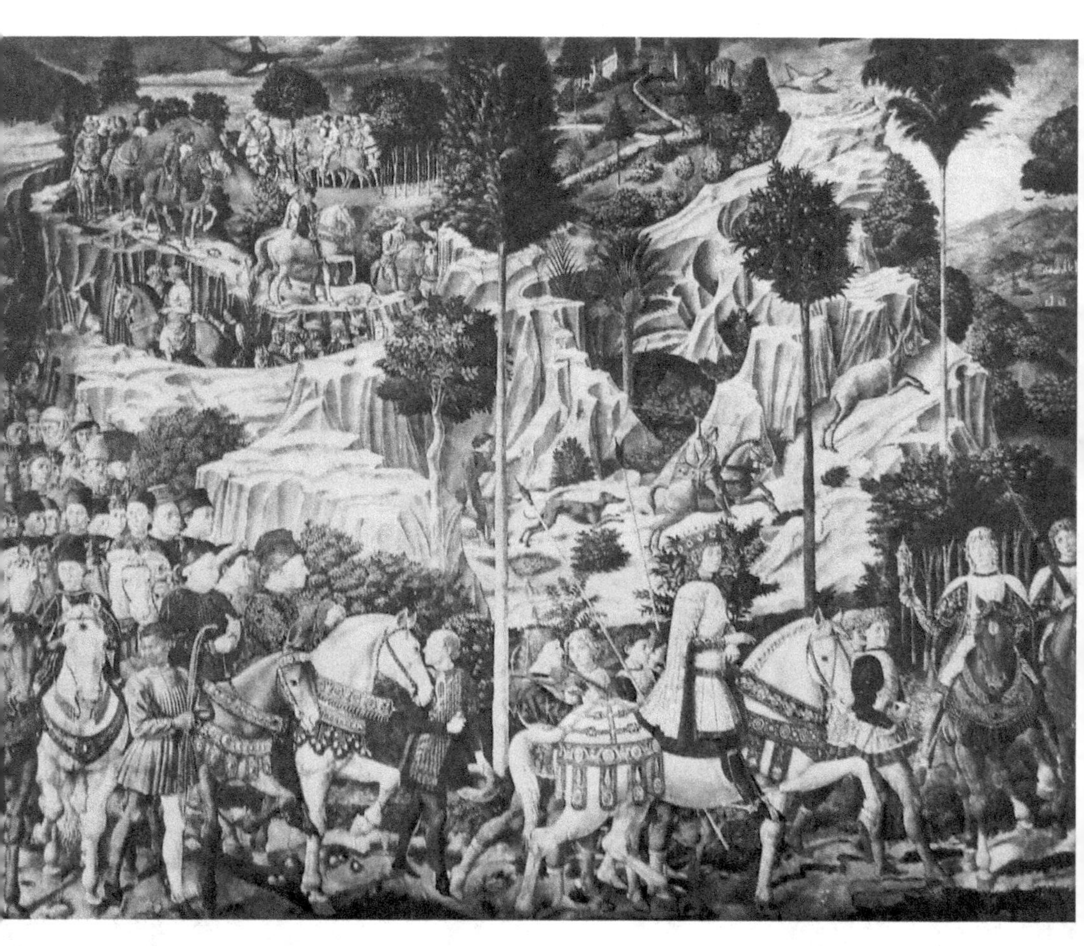

Benozzo Gozzoli, Journey of the Magi

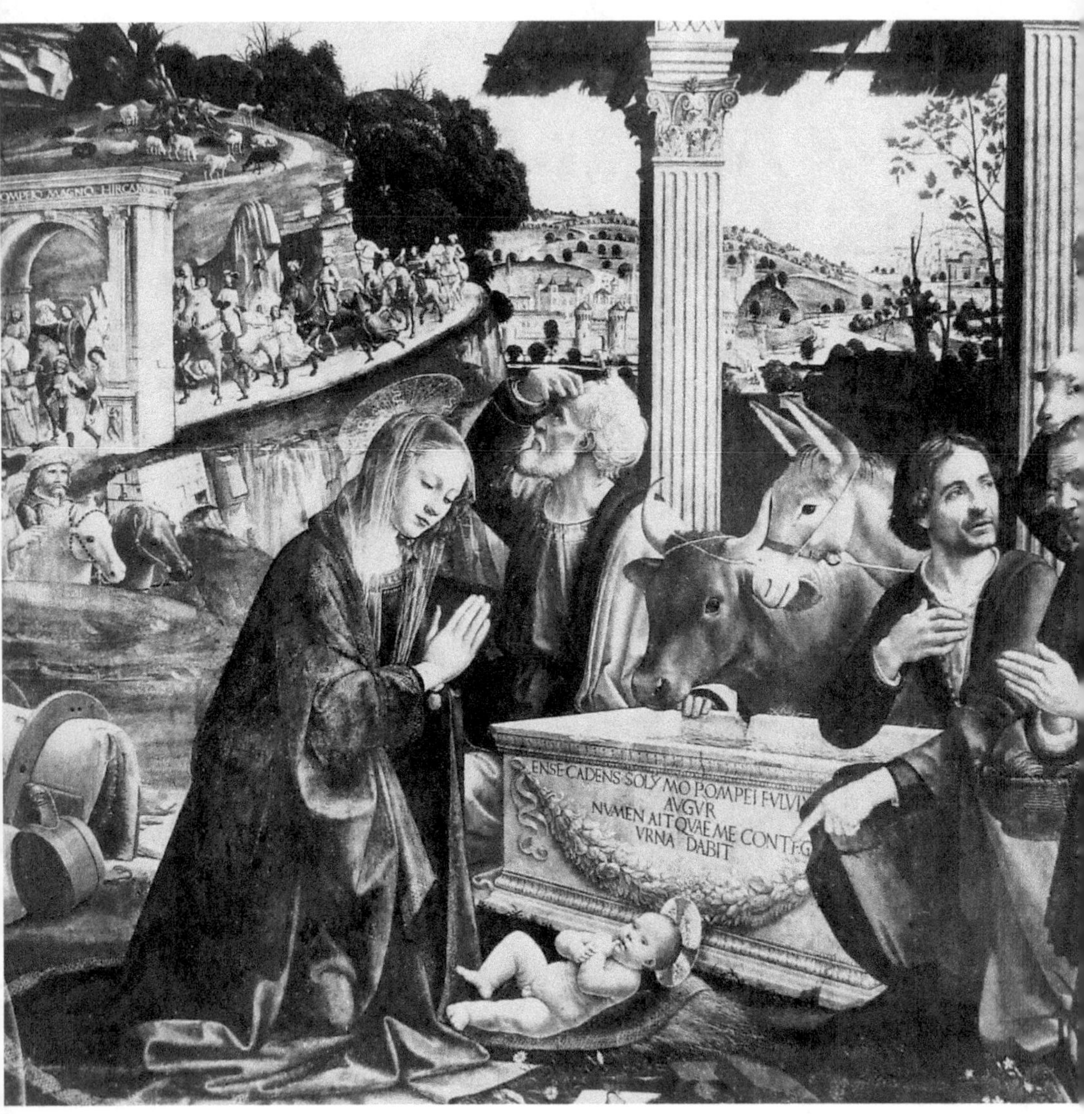

Domenico Ghirlandaio, Adoration of the Shepherds, 1485

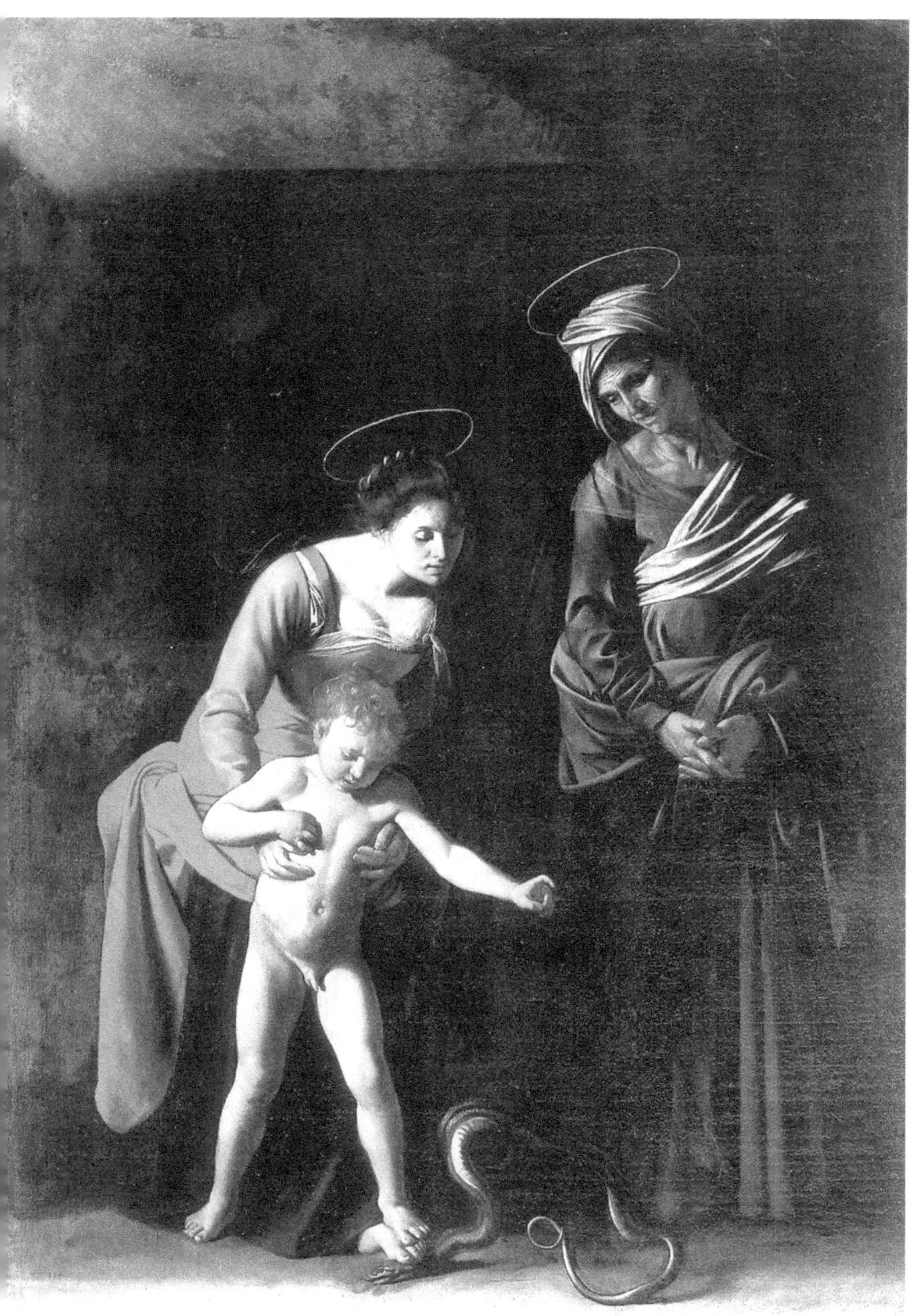

Michelangelo Merisi da Caravaggio, Madonna of the Palafrenieri,
1605-06, Galleria Borghese, Rome

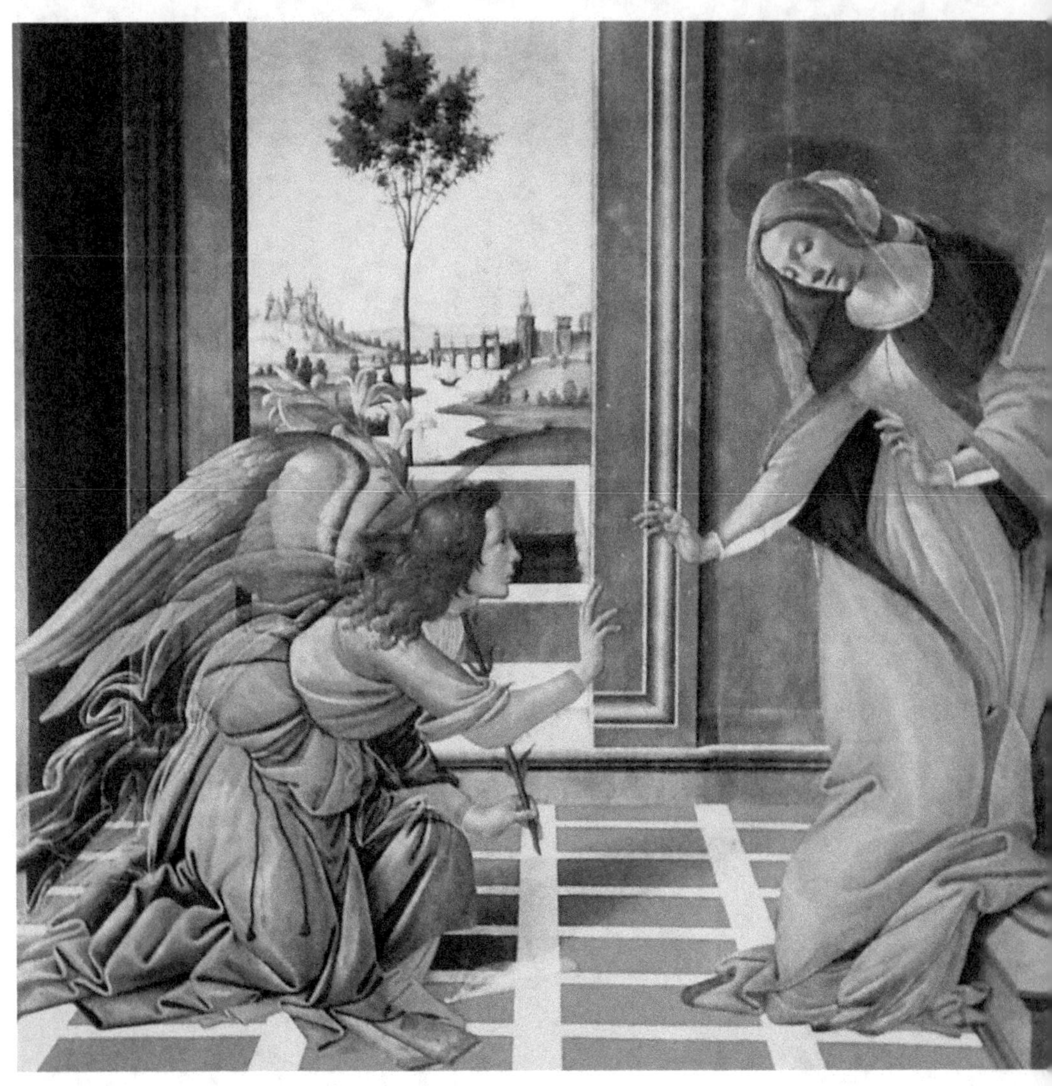

Sandro Botticelli, The Annunciation, Uffizi Gallery, Florence

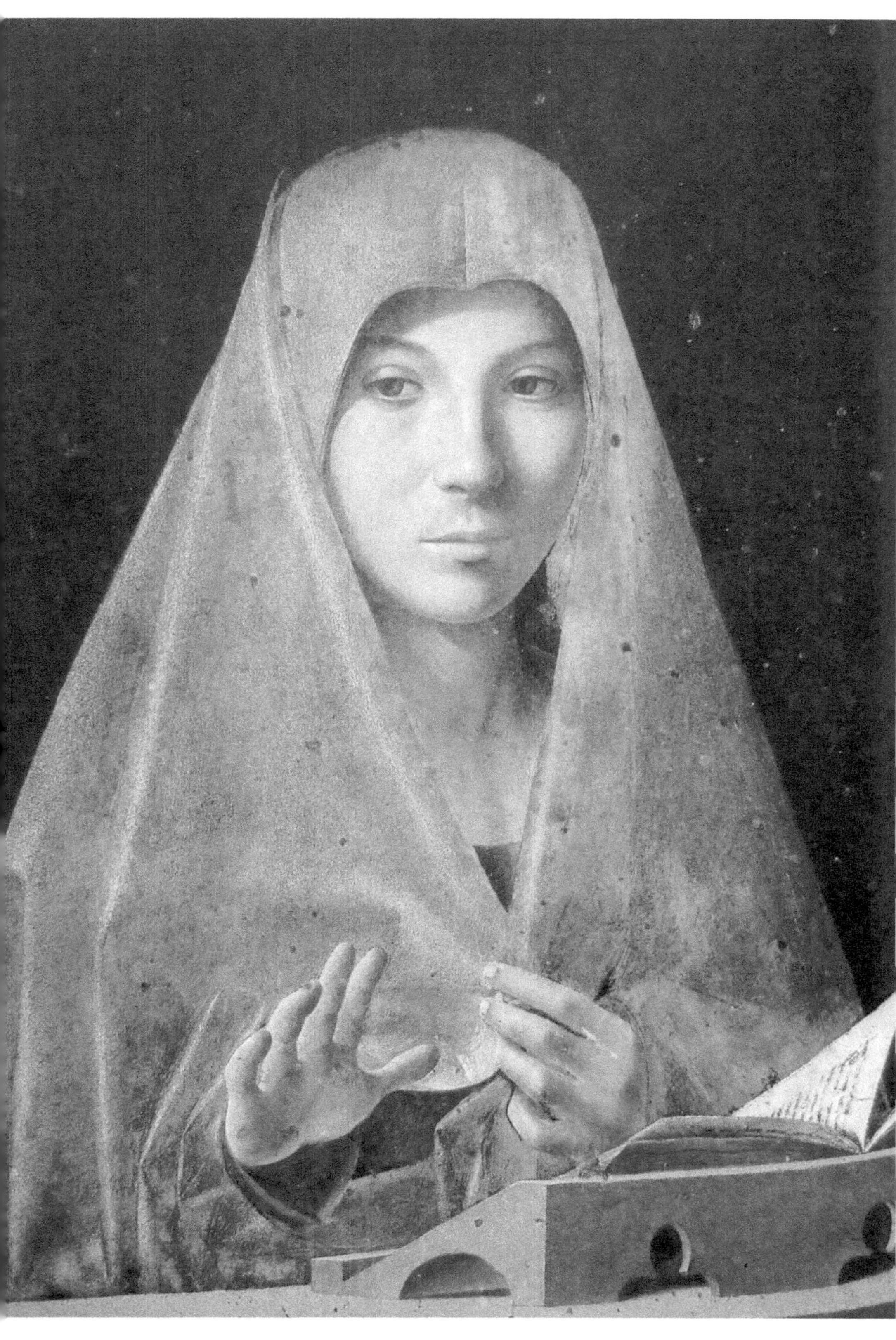

Antonello da Messina, The Virgin of the Annunciation, 1475, Palermo

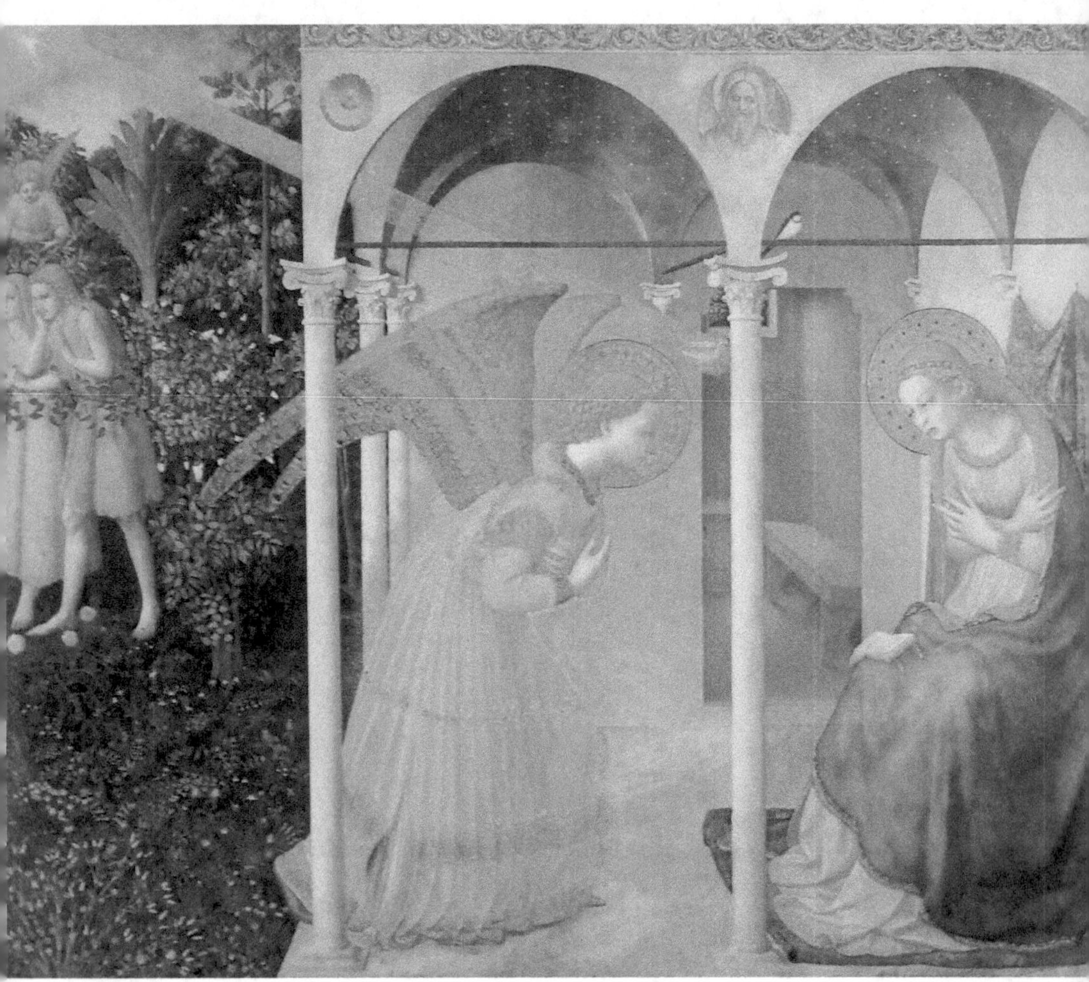

Fra Angelico, Annunciation, Prado, Madrid

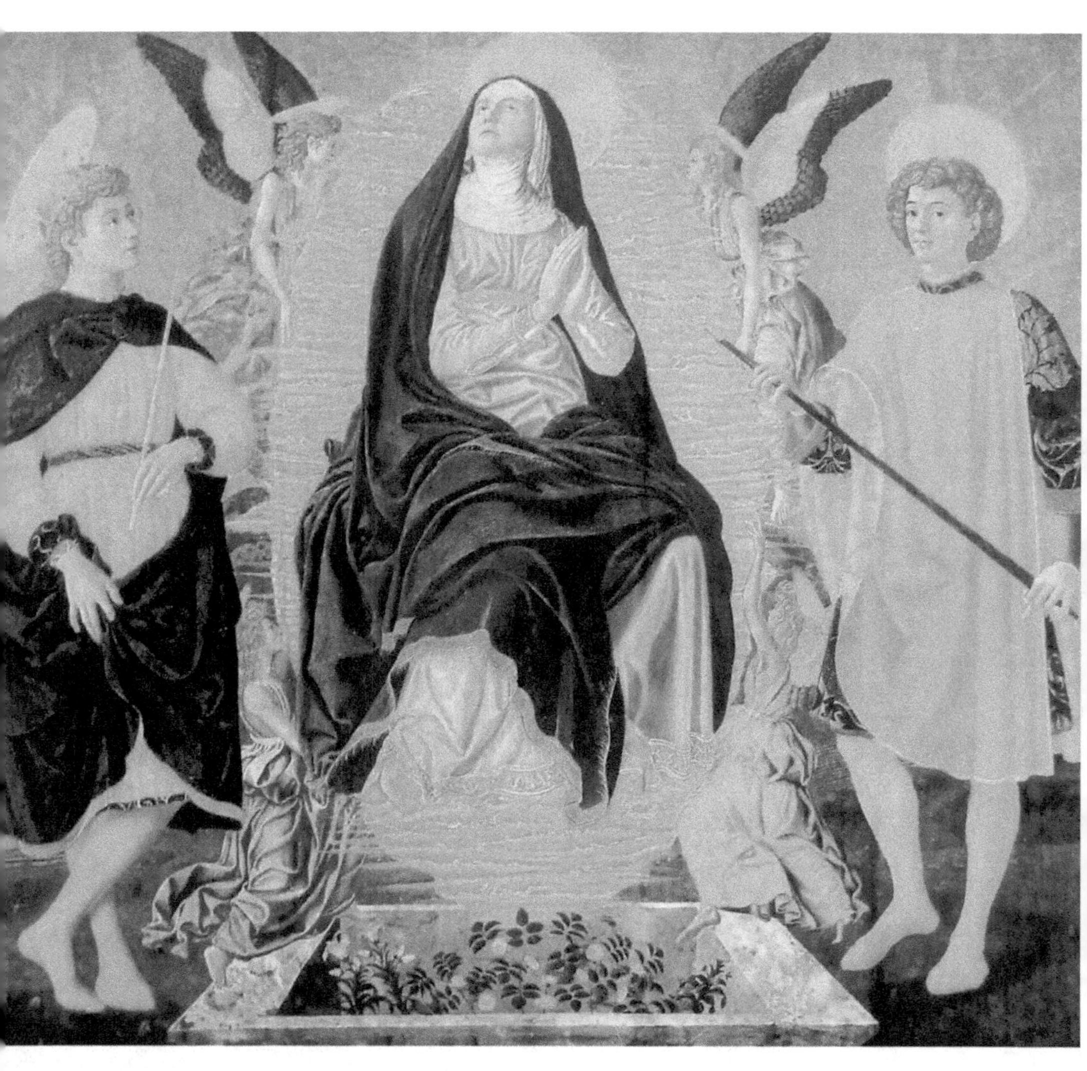

Andrea del Castagno, Assumption, Berlin

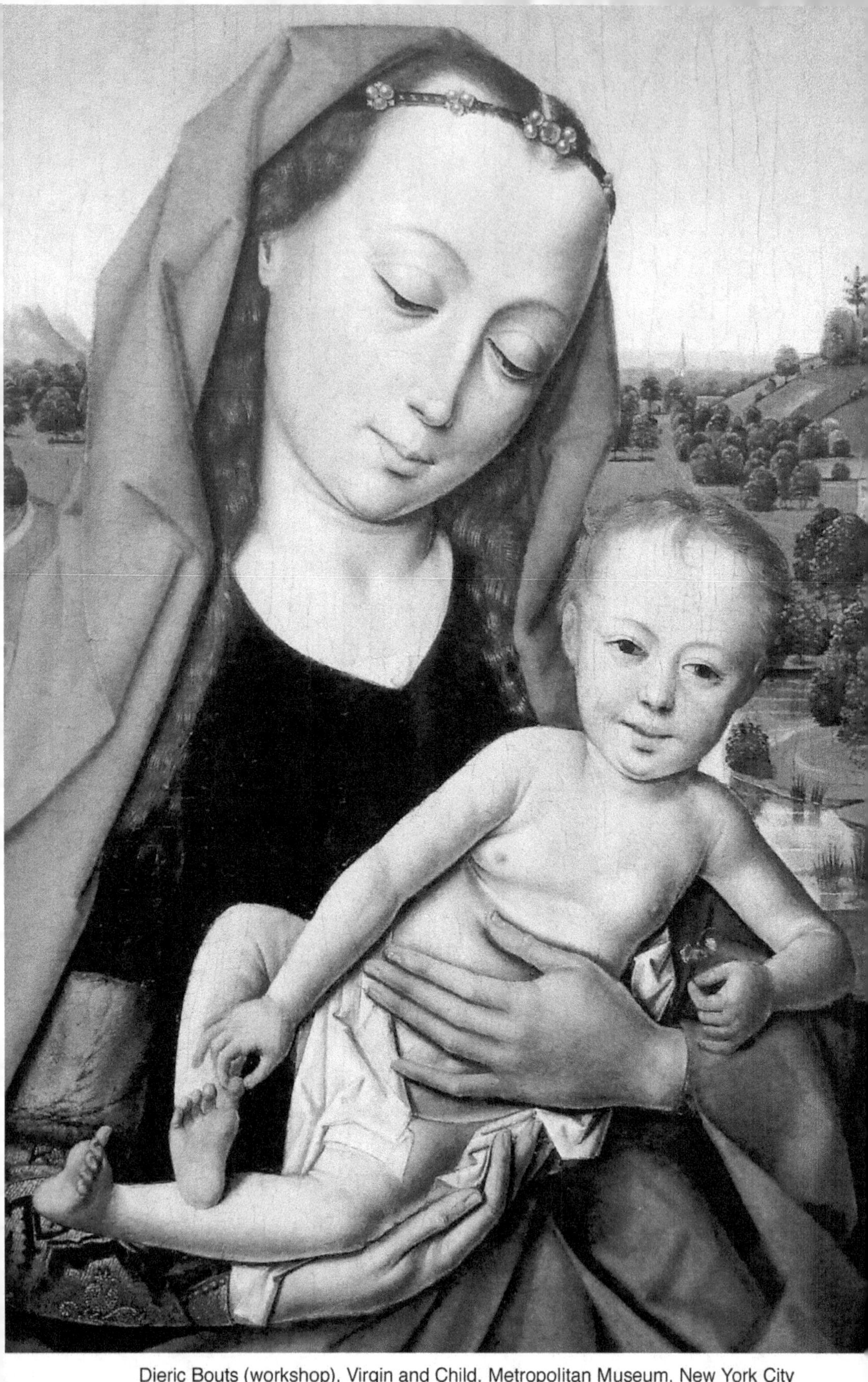

Dieric Bouts (workshop), Virgin and Child, Metropolitan Museum, New York City

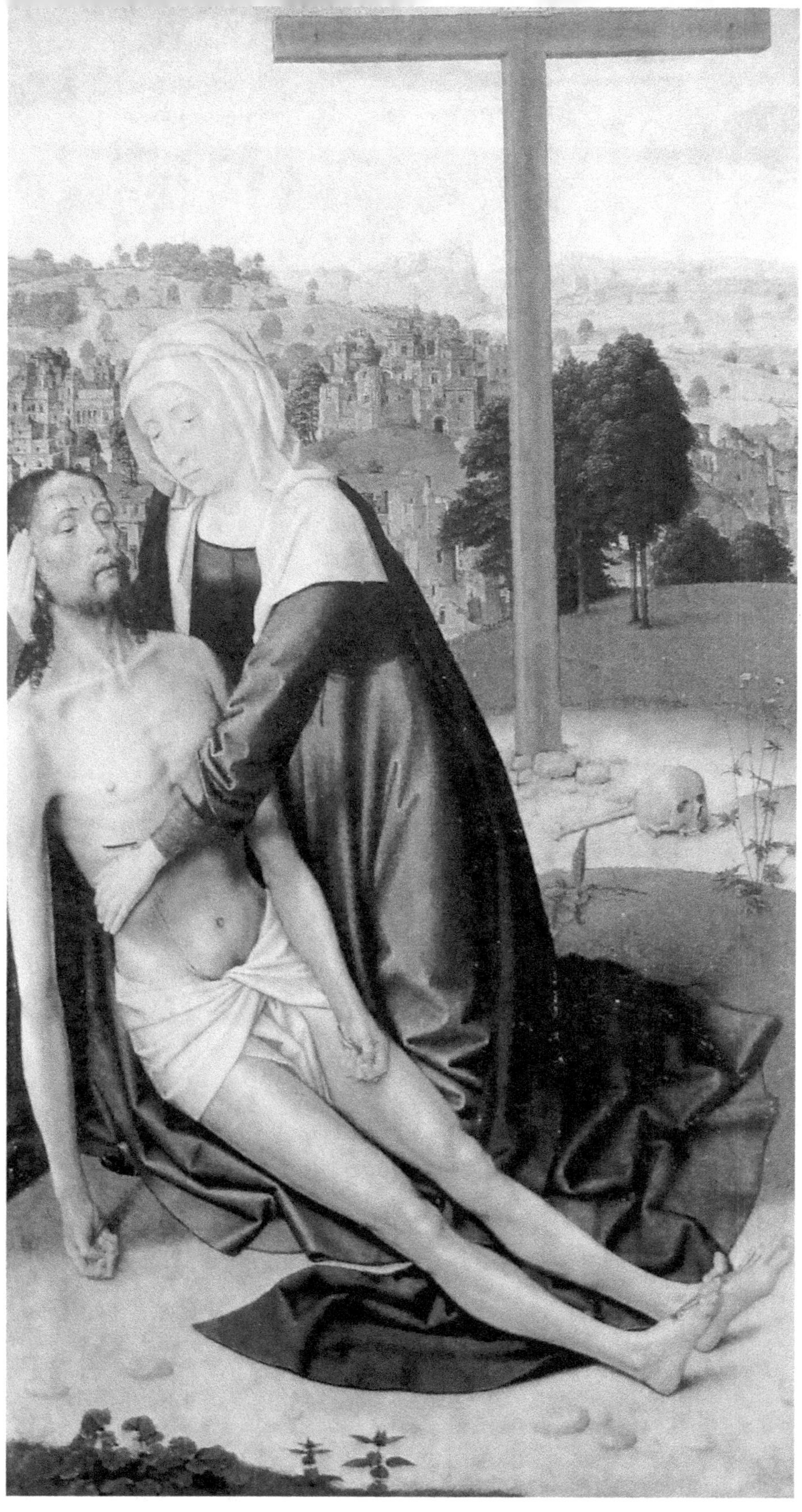

Gerard David, Pietà, Winterhur

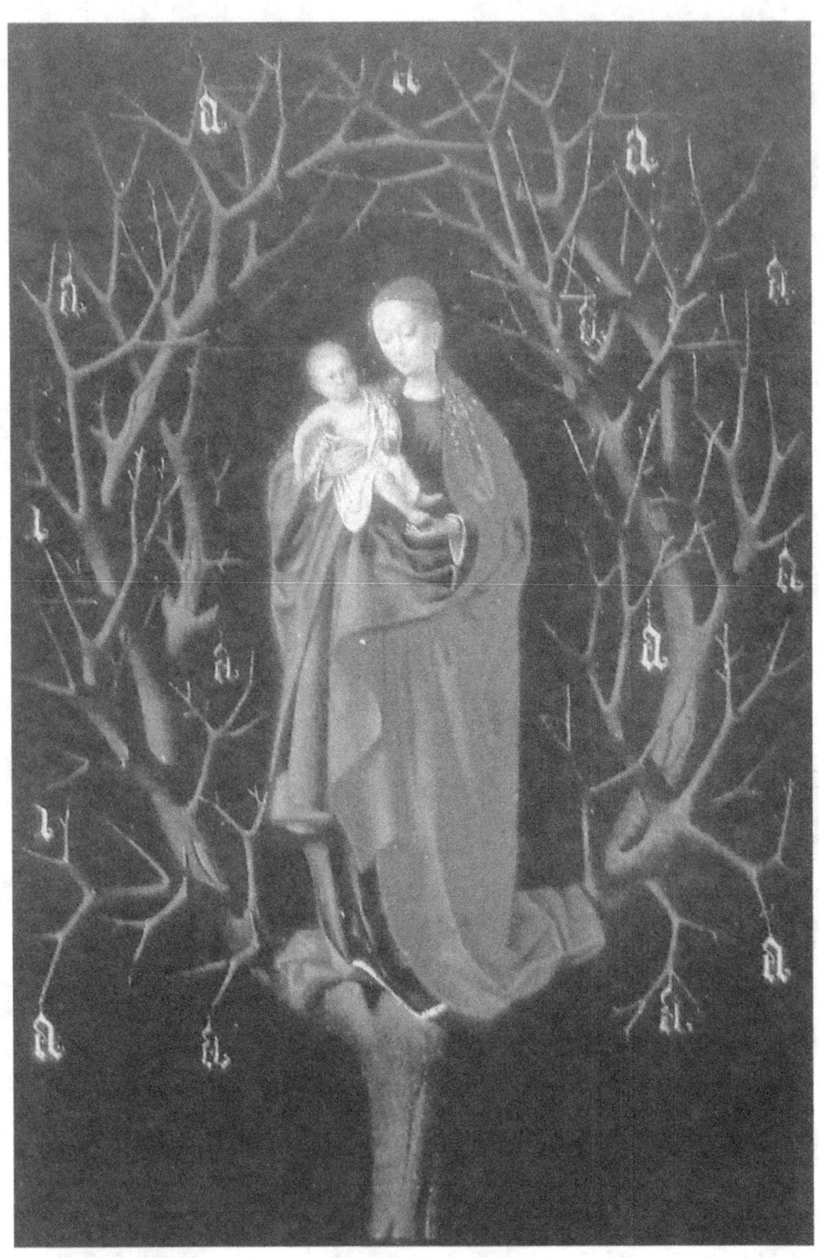

Petrus Christus, Madonna In a Barren Tree, 1450,
Prado, Madrid

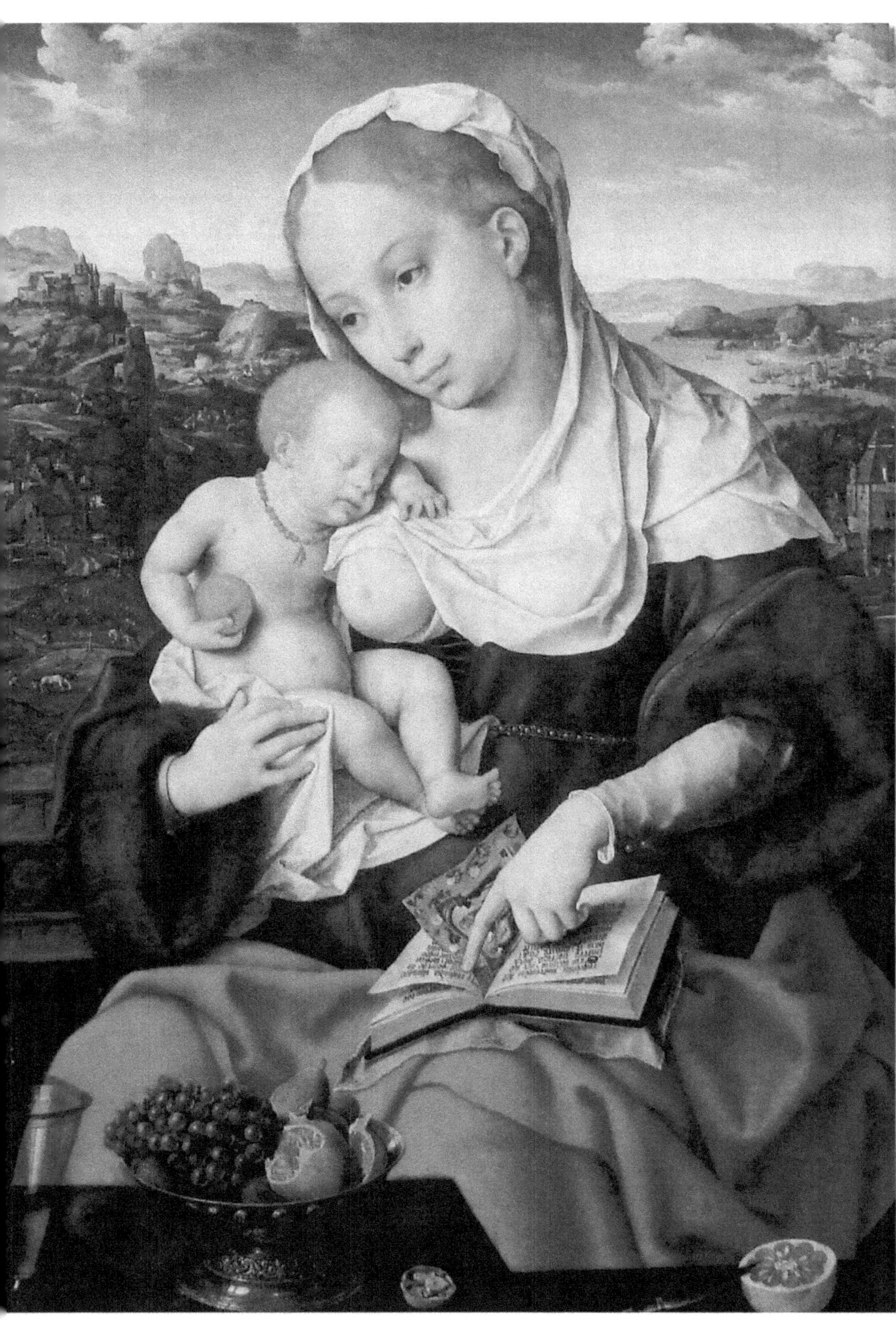

Joos van Cleve, Madonna and Child, Metropolitan Museum,
New York City

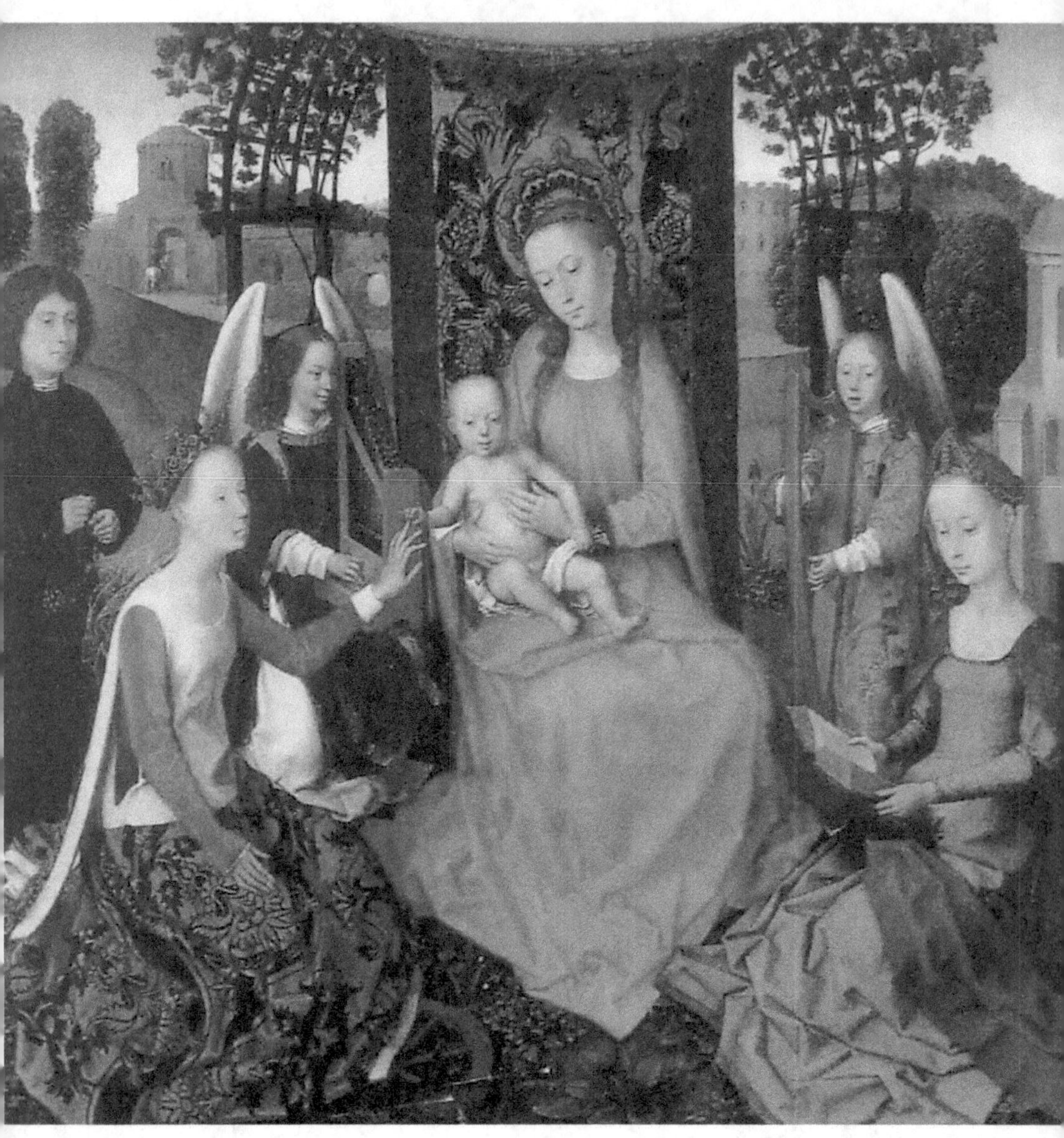

Hans Memling, The Mystic Marriage of St Catherine, Metropolitan
Museum, New York City

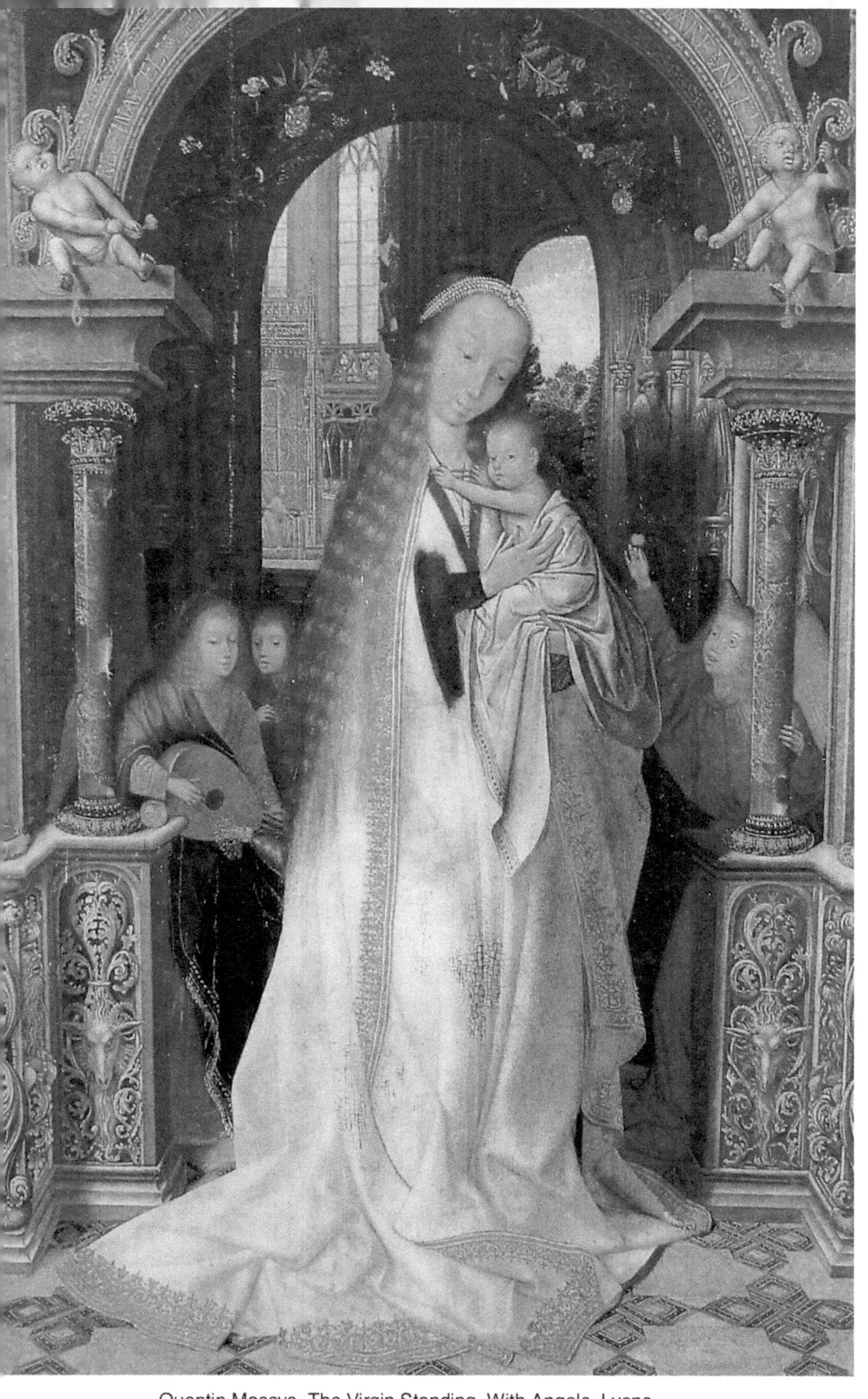

Quentin Massys, The Virgin Standing, With Angels, Lyons

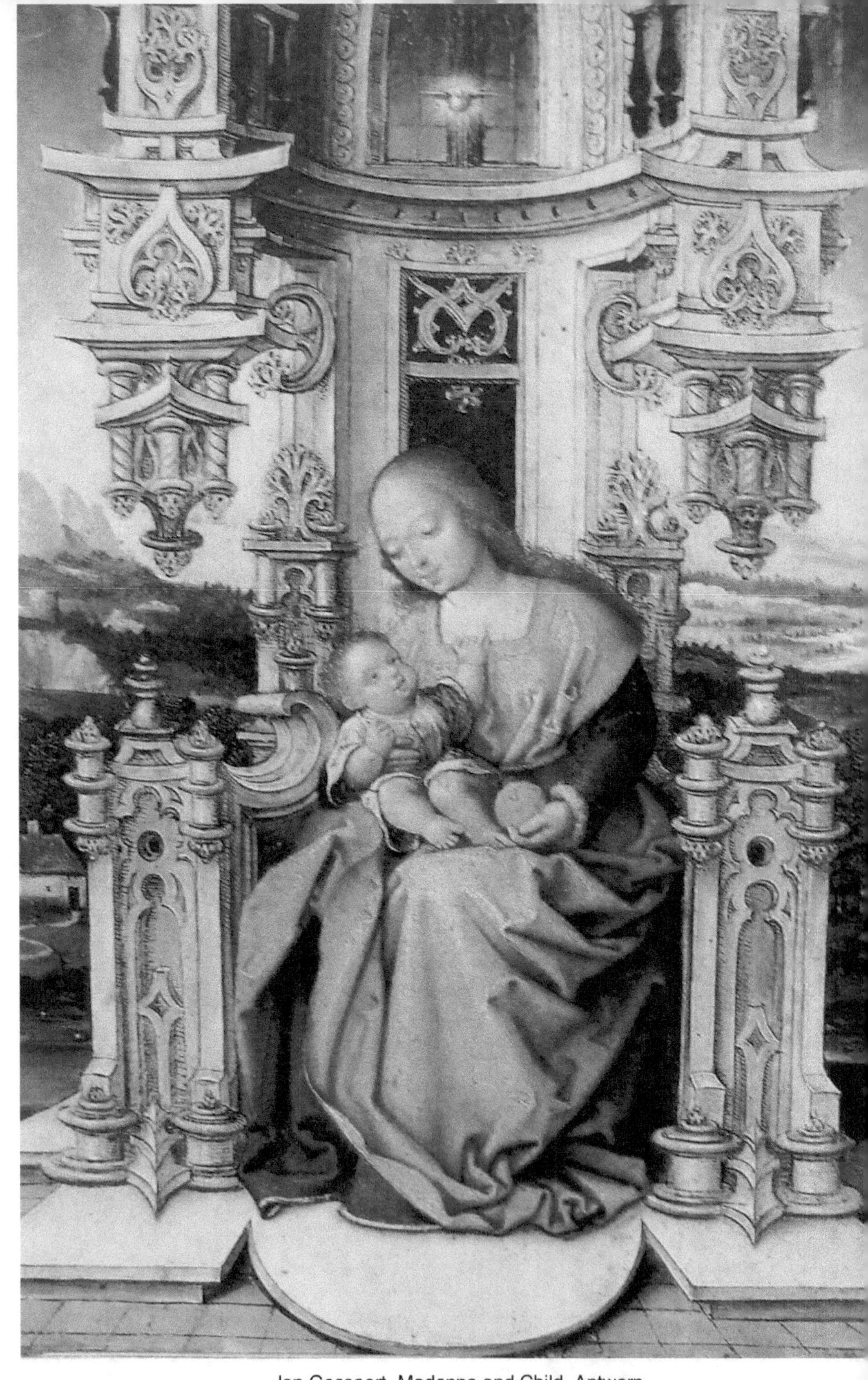

Jan Gossaert, Madonna and Child, Antwerp

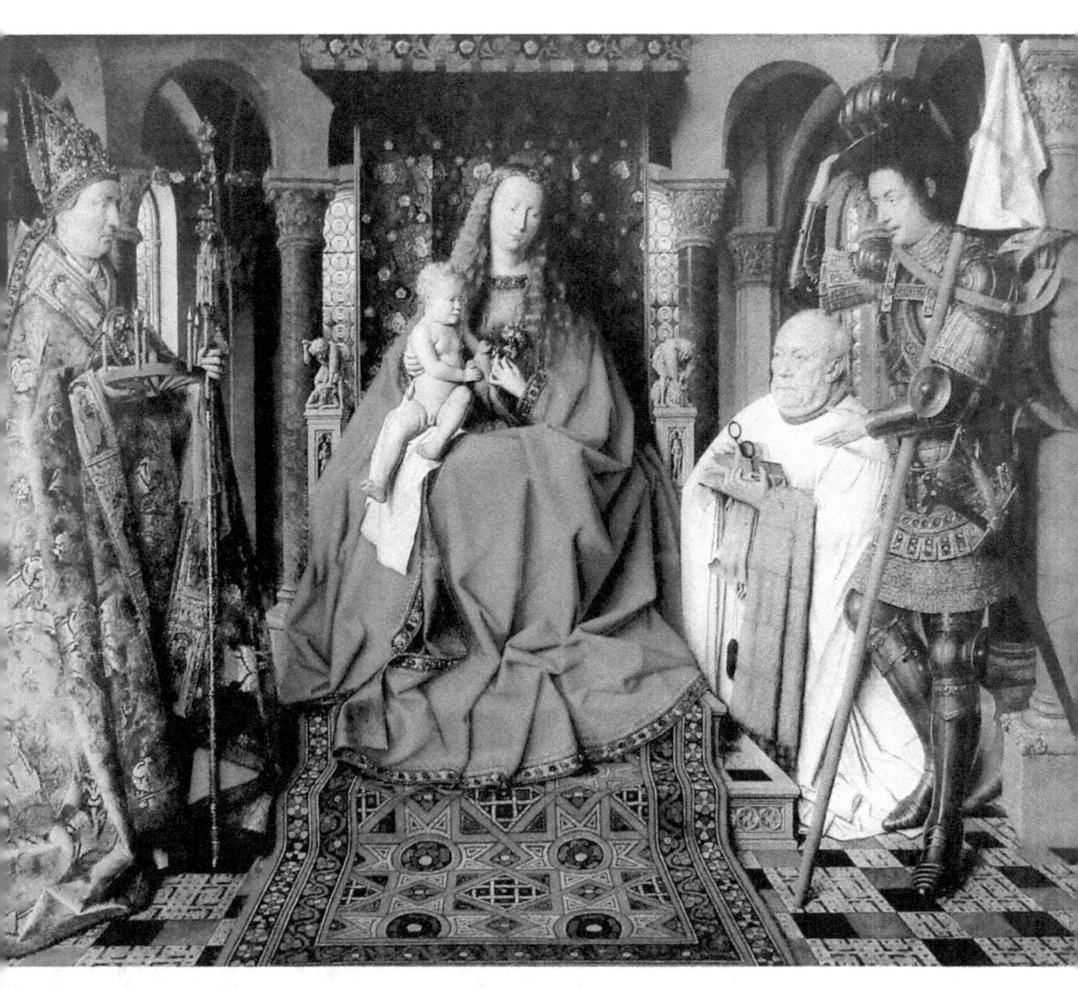

Jan van Eyck, The Paele Madonna, 1436, Bruges

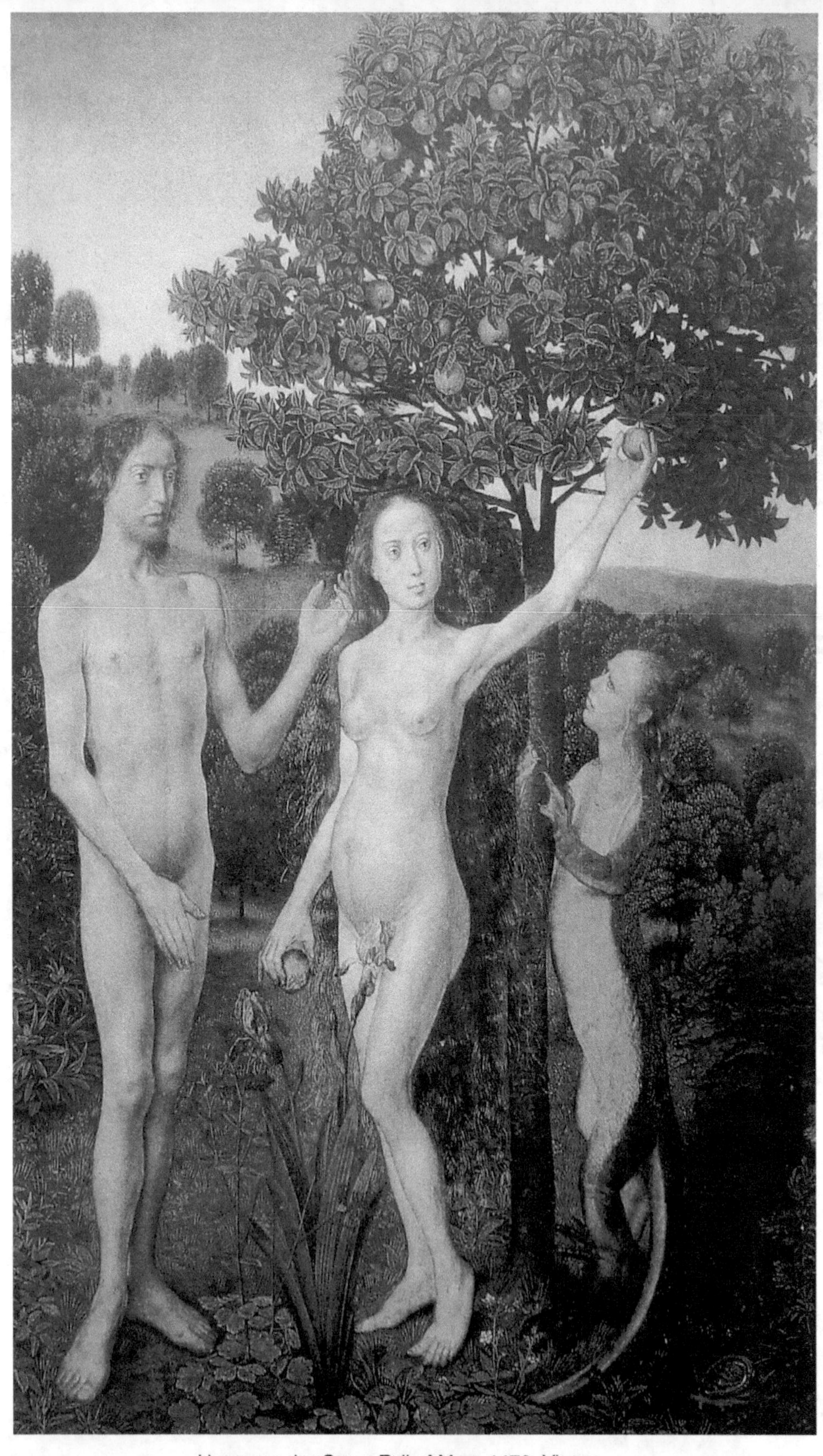

Hugo van der Goes, Fall of Man, 1470, Vienna

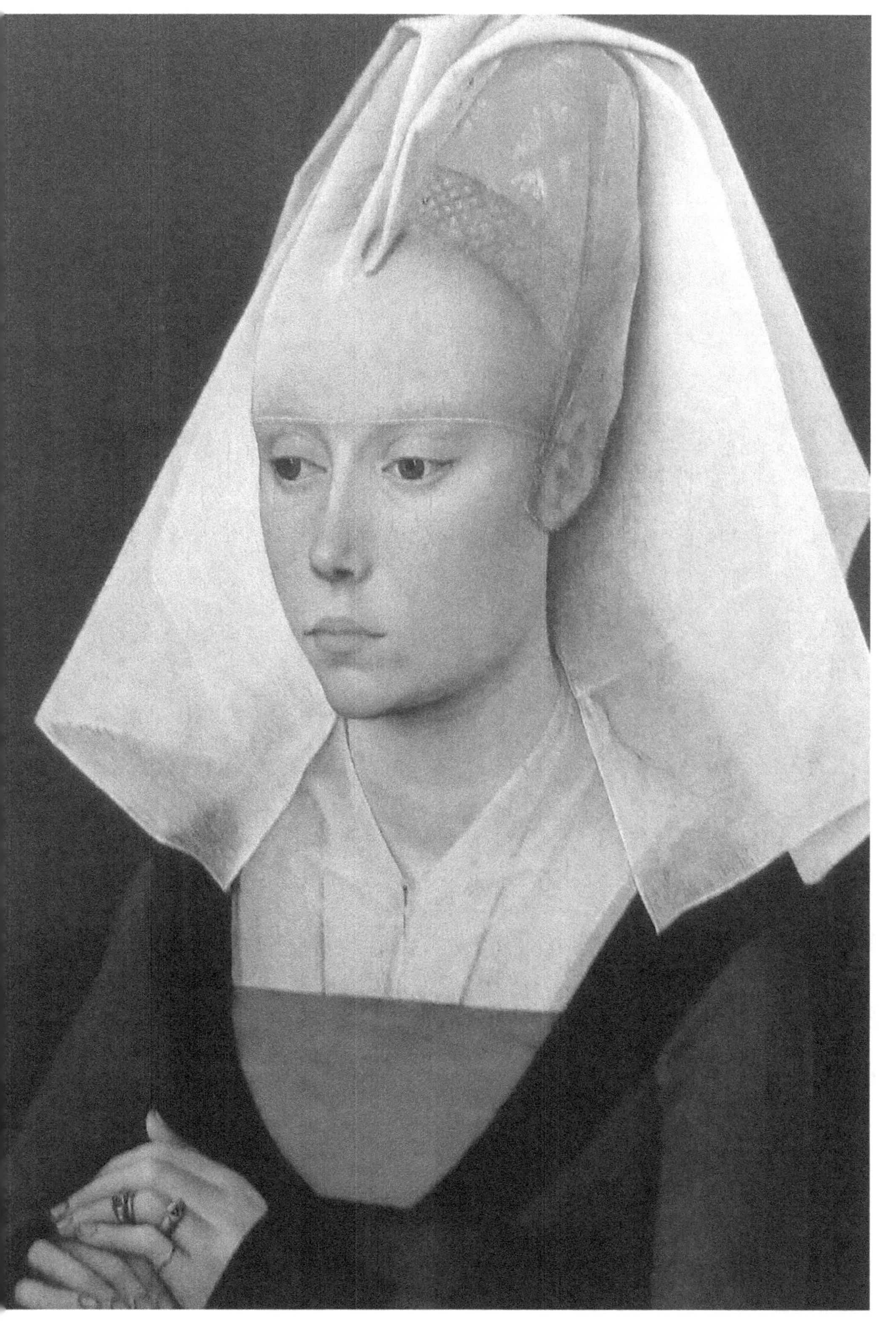

Rogier van der Weyden, Woman Praying, detail, National Gallery, London

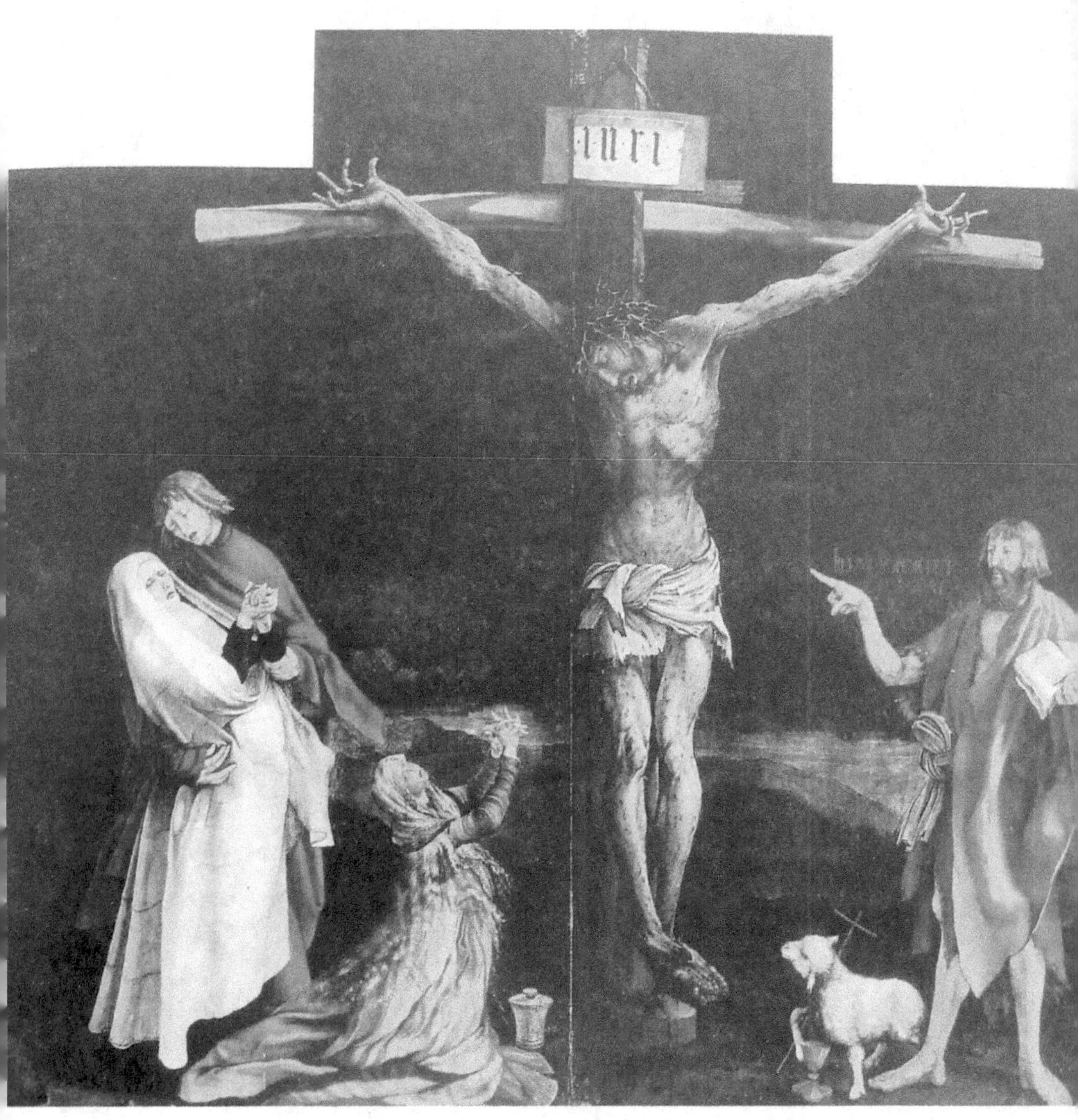

Matthias Grünewald, Crucifixion, Isenheim Altarpiece

NOTES ON WORKS

THE ANSIDEI MADONNA.
(In the National Gallery, London)

Better than any other picture by Raphael, this important altar-piece shows the precociousness of Raphael's genius, for it was painted at Perugia in 1506, when the master had scarcely passed into the twenty-third year of his life. He had then just returned from Florence, but, probably to humour his patrons, the Ansidei family, he reverted in this picture once again to the formal manner of his second master, Perugino. The "Ansidei Madonna" has the distinction of being the most costly picture at the National Gallery – it was purchased in 1885 from the Duke of Marlborough for £70,000.

THE MADONNA DEL GRAN DUCA
(In the Pitti Palace, Florence)

This picture, remarkable for the effective simplicity of its design and for the purity of the Virgin's face, derives the name by which it is commonly known from the fact that it was bought in 1799 by the Grand Duke Ferdinand III. from a poor widow, and held by him in such esteem that he would never part from it and always took it with him on his travels. At one time it was actually credited with the power of working miracles. It is one of the first works of Raphael's Florentine period, and now hangs in the Pitti Palace, Florence.

THE MADONNA DELLA SEDIA
(In the Pitti Palace, Florence)

The Madonna "of the Chair," one of the most characteristic and deservedly popular of Raphael's numerous versions of the Virgin and Child *motif*, belongs to the master's full maturity, and was painted during his sojourn in Rome, at the time when he was occupied with the stupendous task of decorating the *Stanze* of the Vatican. It would be difficult to find in the whole history of art a more pleasing solution of the problem presented by a figure composition in the round. The picture is now in the Pitti Palace, Florence.

LA BELLE JARDINIÈRE
(In the Louvre)

"La Belle Jardinière" is a magnificent example of Raphael's Florentine style, which came from his being influenced by Leonardo da Vinci when at Florence (see the triangular composition). The Virgin's mantle was probably finished by Ridolfo Ghirlandaio; other parts – the hands and the feet – are hardly finished; nevertheless it is one of the finest, most expressive, and touching Madonnas by the Master.

THE MADONNA OF THE TOWER
(In the National Gallery, London)

This beautiful painting, which the National Gallery owes to
the generosity of Miss Eva Mackintosh, who presented it to the
nation in 1906, was at one time in the collection of the Duc
d'Orléans. The late owner was fortunate in securing this
unquestionably genuine masterpiece at the Rogers' sale in 1856
for 480 guineas. It was painted about 1512; and a copy of it by
Sassoferrato is in the Leichtenburg collection in St. Petersburg.

POPE JULIUS II.
(In the Uffizi Gallery, Florence)

Raphael's greatness as a portrait painter may be judged from
his painting of his first papal patron, the warlike Giuliano della
Rovere, who as Pope adopted the name of Julius II. This portrait
has more than the perfection of form, colour, and execution that is
ever associated with Raphael's name. It has depth of character,
dignity, and serious concentration of thought, and is worthy of
being placed beside Velazquez's immortal portrait of Pope
Innocent X. The picture is at the Uffizi Gallery, but replicas are to
be found at the Palazzo Pitti and at the National Gallery.

PUTTO WITH GARLAND
(In the Academy of St. Luca, Rome)

The fresco of a *putto,* now at the Academy of St. Luca in Rome,
is the only fragment that is left to the world of all the decorative
work executed by Raphael for the corridor leading from the

famous *Stanze* of the Vatican to the Belvedere. It probably belonged to a shield bearing the papal arms, and is a graceful and characteristic example of the master's treatment of the form of children which he loved to introduce into his compositions.

PORTRAIT OF RAPHAEL
(In the Uffizi Gallery, Florence)

Though much "restored" and over-painted – and not by the most competent hands – the portrait of Raphael in the *Sala dei Pittori* at the Uffizi, the Walhalla of pictorial fame, is undoubtedly painted by the master himself, at the age of about twenty-three, when his features had lost none of the almost girlish charm and delicacy of which we are told by contemporary writers. In time the portrait stands midway between Timoteo Viti's charming drawing of his "apprentice," the boy Raphael, at the Oxford University Galleries, and Sebastiano del Piombo's portrait of the "Prince of Painters" at the Buda-Pesth Museum.

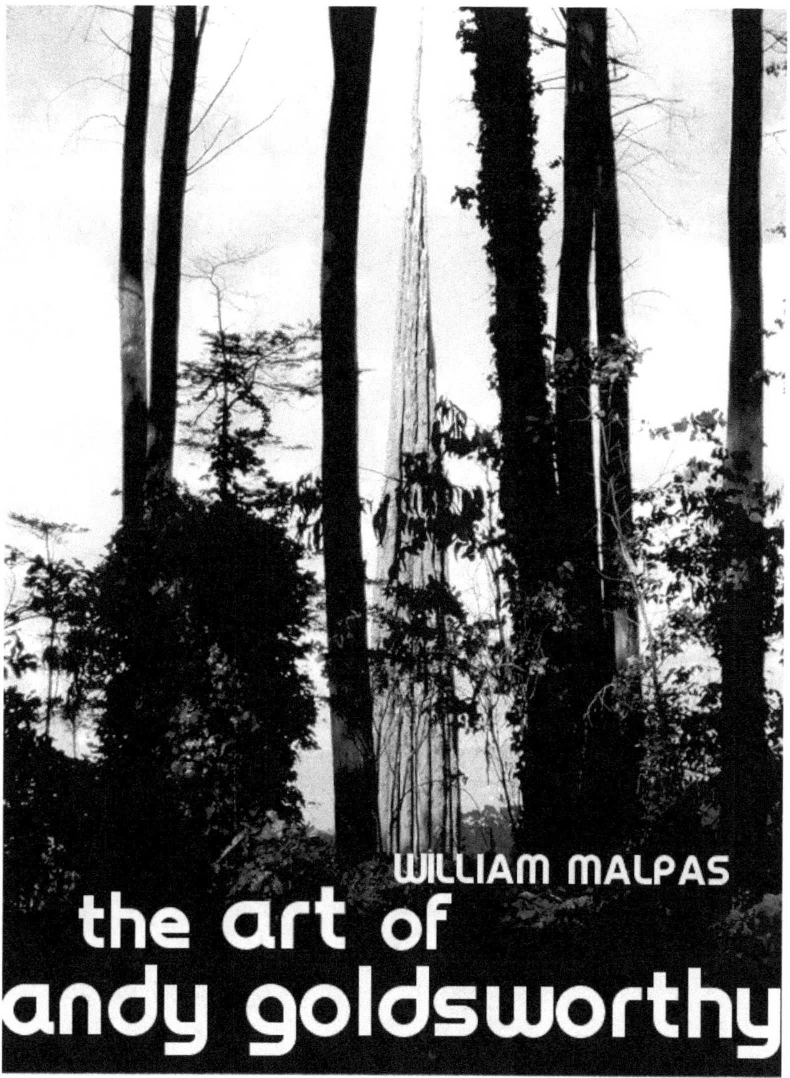

This is the most comprehensive and detailed account of the art of Andy Goldsworthy available.

This study of Andy Goldsworthy discusses all of Goldsworthy's major exhibitions, books and projects, including the *Sheepfolds* project; *Garden of Stones* in New York; TV and dance collaborations; and the books *Wood, Stone, Time* and *Passage*. William Malpas surveys all of Goldsworthy's output, and analyzes his relation with other land artists such as Robert Smithson, the Christos, Walter de Maria, Chris Drury, Richard Long and David Nash; women sculptors; sculpture in the modern era; and Goldsworthy's place in the contemporary British art scene.

The book has been updated and revised for this new edition.

ISBN 9781861714107 Pbk   ISBN 9781861714114 Hbk
Fully illustrated   www.crmoon.com

MAURICE SENDAK

& the art of children's book illustration

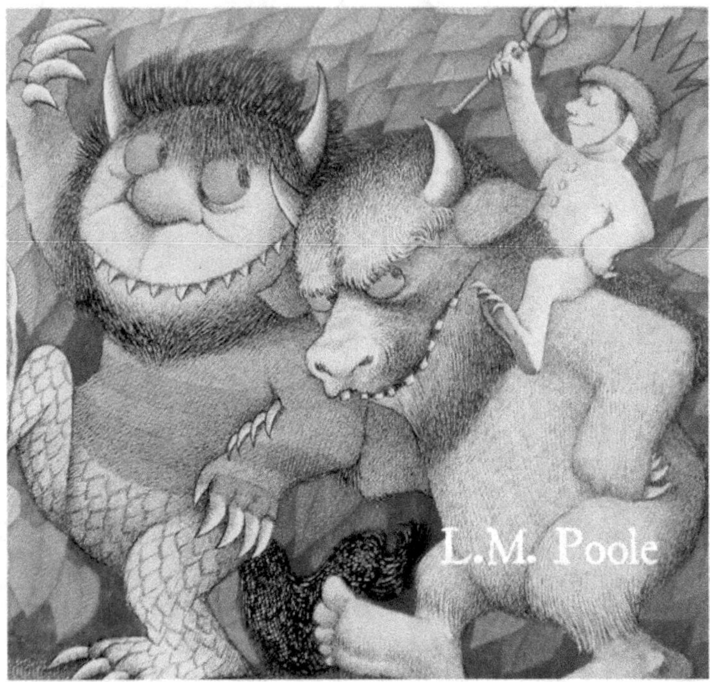

Maurice Sendak is the widely acclaimed American children's book author and illustrator. This critical study focuses on his famous trilogy, *Where the Wild Things Are, In the Night Kitchen* and *Outside Over There*, as well as the early works and Sendak's superb depictions of the Grimm Brothers' fairy tales in *The Juniper Tree*. L.M. Poole begins with a chapter on children's book illustration, in particular the treatment of fairy tales. Sendak's work is situated within the history of children's book illustration, and he is compared with many contemporary authors.

Fully illustrated. The book has been revised and updated for this edition.
ISBN 9781861714282 Pbk   ISBN 9781861713469 Hbk

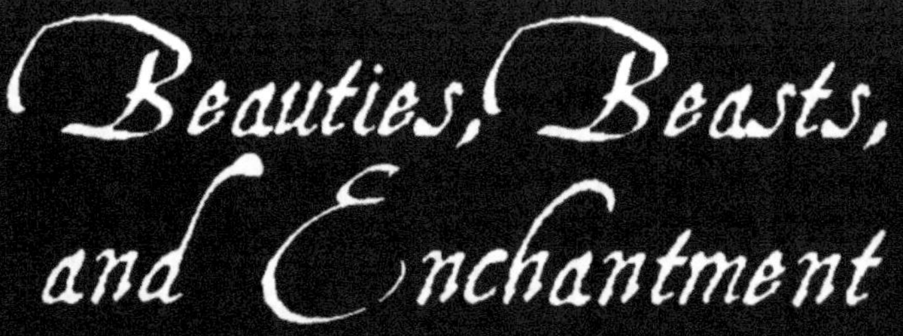

CLASSIC FRENCH FAIRY TALES

Translated and with an Introduction
by Jack Zipes

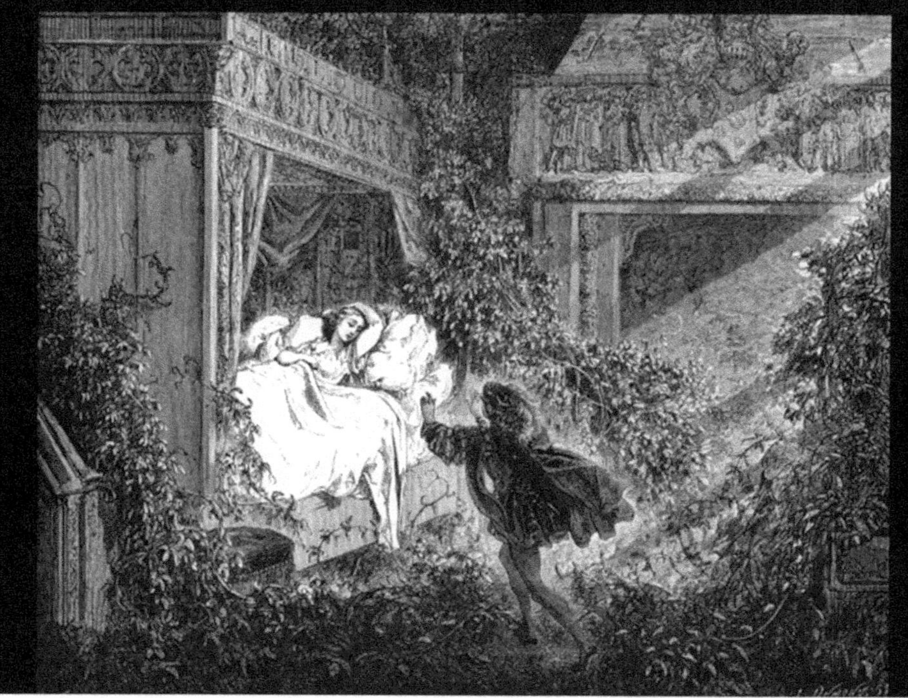

A collection of 36 classic French fairy tales translated by renowned writer Jack Zipes.
Cinderella, Beauty and the Beast, Sleeping Beauty and *Little Red Riding Hood* are among the
classic fairy tales in this amazing book.
Includes illustrations from fairy tale collections.
Jack Zipes has written and published widely on fairy tales.

'Terrific... a succulent array of 17th and 18th century 'salon' fairy tales'
- *The New York Times Book Review*

'These tales are adventurous, thrilling in a way fairy tales are meant to be... The translation
from the French is modern, happily free of archaic and hyperbolic language... a fine and
sophisticated collection' - *New York Tribune*

'Enjoyable to read... a unique collection of French regional folklore' - *Library Journal*

'Charming stories accompanied by attractive pen-and-ink drawings' - *Chattanooga Times*

Introduction and illustrations   612pp.   ISBN 9781861712510 Pbk   ISBN 9781861713193 Hbk

CRESCENT MOON PUBLISHING

web: www.crmoon.com e-mail: cresmopub@yahoo.co.uk

ARTS, PAINTING, SCULPTURE

The Art of Andy Goldsworthy
Andy Goldsworthy: Touching Nature
Andy Goldsworthy in Close-Up
Andy Goldsworthy: Pocket Guide
Andy Goldsworthy In America
Land Art: A Complete Guide
The Art of Richard Long
Richard Long: Pocket Guide
Land Art In the UK
Land Art in Close-Up
Land Art In the U.S.A.
Land Art: Pocket Guide
Installation Art in Close-Up
Minimal Art and Artists In the 1960s and After
Colourfield Painting
Land Art DVD, TV documentary
Andy Goldsworthy DVD, TV documentary
The Erotic Object: Sexuality in Sculpture From Prehistory to the Present Day
Sex in Art: Pornography and Pleasure in Painting and Sculpture
Postwar Art
Sacred Gardens: The Garden in Myth, Religion and Art
Glorification: Religious Abstraction in Renaissance and 20th Century Art
Early Netherlandish Painting
Leonardo da Vinci
Piero della Francesca
Giovanni Bellini
Fra Angelico: Art and Religion in the Renaissance
Mark Rothko: The Art of Transcendence
Frank Stella: American Abstract Artist
Jasper Johns
Brice Marden
Alison Wilding: The Embrace of Sculpture
Vincent van Gogh: Visionary Landscapes
Eric Gill: Nuptials of God
Constantin Brancusi: Sculpting the Essence of Things
Max Beckmann
Caravaggio
Gustave Moreau
Egon Schiele: Sex and Death In Purple Stockings
Delizioso Fotografico Fervore: Works In Process 1
Sacro Cuore: Works In Process 2
The Light Eternal: J.M.W. Turner
The Madonna Glorified: Karen Arthurs

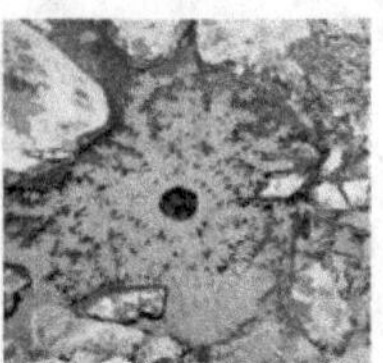
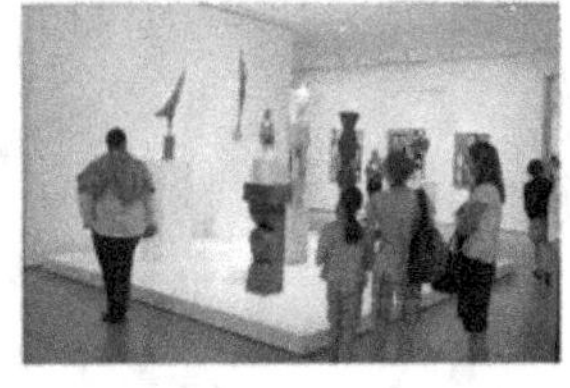
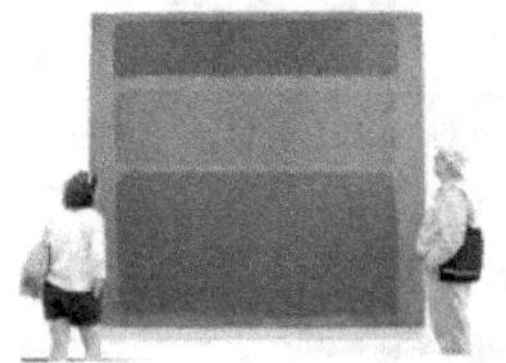
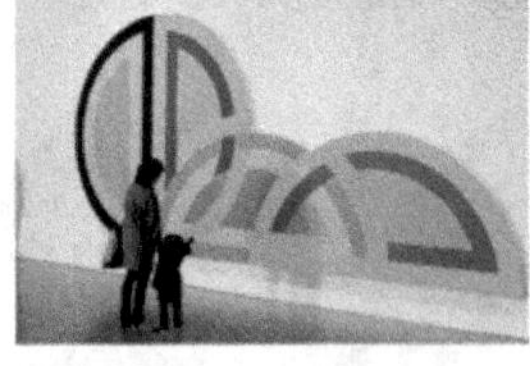
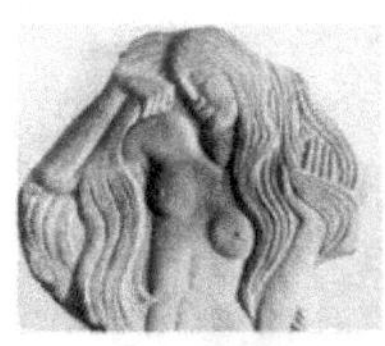
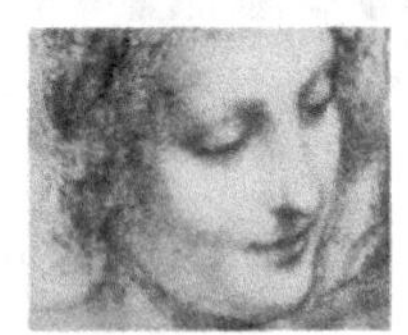
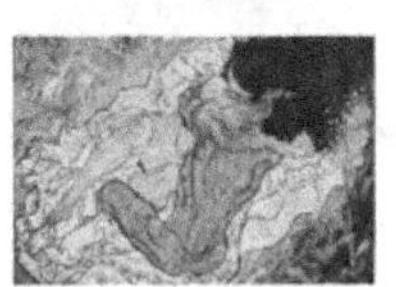
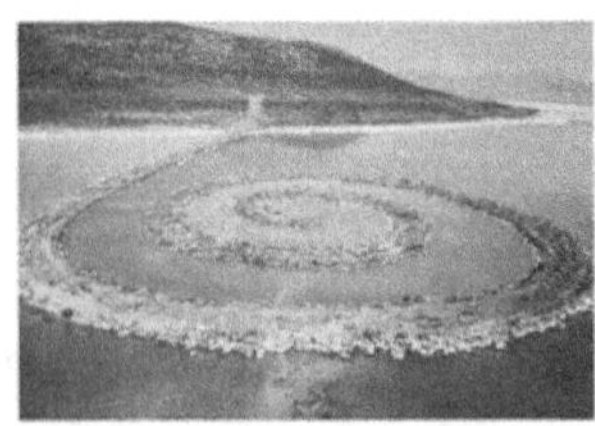

LITERATURE

J.R.R. Tolkien: The Books, The Films, The Whole Cultural Phenomenon
J.R.R. Tolkien: Pocket Guide
Tolkien's Heroic Quest
The *Earthsea* Books of Ursula Le Guin
Beauties, Beasts and Enchantment: Classic French Fairy Tales
German Popular Stories by the Brothers Grimm
Philip Pullman and *His Dark Materials*
Sexing Hardy: Thomas Hardy and Feminism
Thomas Hardy's *Tess of the d'Urbervilles*
Thomas Hardy's *Jude the Obscure*
Thomas Hardy: The Tragic Novels
Love and Tragedy: Thomas Hardy
The Poetry of Landscape in Hardy
Wessex Revisited: Thomas Hardy and John Cowper Powys
Wolfgang Iser: Essays and Interviews
Petrarch, Dante and the Troubadours
Maurice Sendak and the Art of Children's Book Illustration
Andrea Dworkin
Cixous, Irigaray, Kristeva: The *Jouissance* of French Feminism
Julia Kristeva: Art, Love, Melancholy, Philosophy, Semiotics and Psychoanalysis
Hélene Cixous I Love You: The *Jouissance* of Writing
Luce Irigaray: Lips, Kissing, and the Politics of Sexual Difference
Peter Redgrove: Here Comes the Flood
Peter Redgrove: Sex-Magic-Poetry-Cornwall
Lawrence Durrell: Between Love and Death, East and West
Love, Culture & Poetry: Lawrence Durrell
Cavafy: Anatomy of a Soul
German Romantic Poetry: Goethe, Novalis, Heine, Hölderlin
Feminism and Shakespeare
Shakespeare: Love, Poetry & Magic
The Passion of D.H. Lawrence
D.H. Lawrence: Symbolic Landscapes
D.H. Lawrence: Infinite Sensual Violence
Rimbaud: Arthur Rimbaud and the Magic of Poetry
The Ecstasies of John Cowper Powys
Sensualism and Mythology: The Wessex Novels of John Cowper Powys
Amorous Life: John Cowper Powys and the Manifestation of Affectivity (H.W. Fawkner)
Postmodern Powys: New Essays on John Cowper Powys (Joe Boulter)
Rethinking Powys: Critical Essays on John Cowper Powys
Paul Bowles & Bernardo Bertolucci
Rainer Maria Rilke
Joseph Conrad: *Heart of Darkness*
In the Dim Void: Samuel Beckett
Samuel Beckett Goes into the Silence
André Gide: Fiction and Fervour
Jackie Collins and the Blockbuster Novel
Blinded By Her Light: The Love-Poetry of Robert Graves
The Passion of Colours: Travels In Mediterranean Lands
Poetic Forms

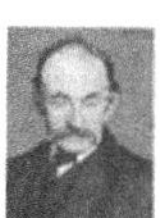
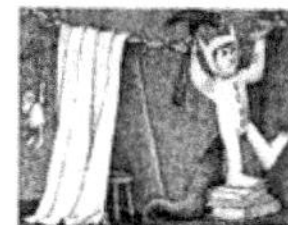
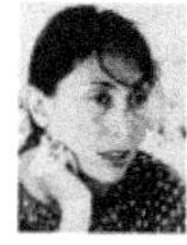
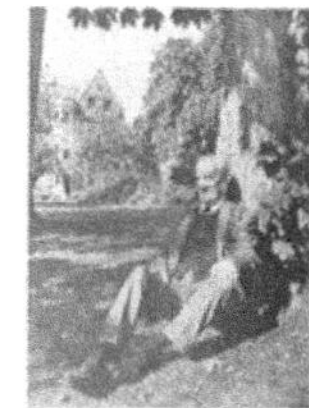
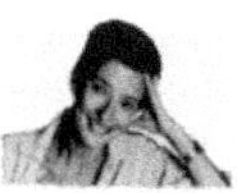
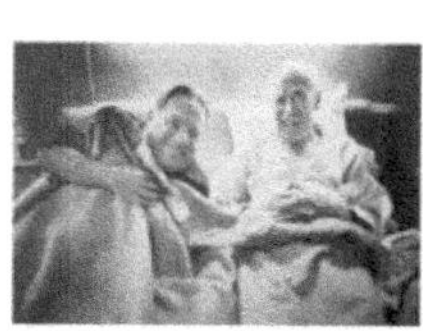
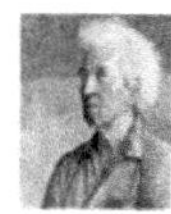
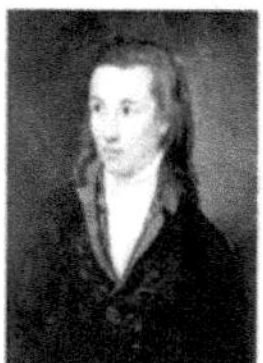

POETRY

Ursula Le Guin: Walking In Cornwall
Peter Redgrove: Here Comes The Flood
Peter Redgrove: Sex-Magic-Poetry-Cornwall
Dante: Selections From the Vita Nuova
Petrarch, Dante and the Troubadours
William Shakespeare: Sonnets
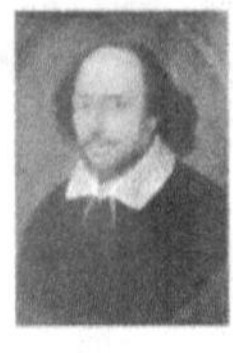
William Shakespeare: Complete Poems
Blinded By Her Light: The Love-Poetry of Robert Graves
Emily Dickinson: Selected Poems
Emily Brontë: Poems
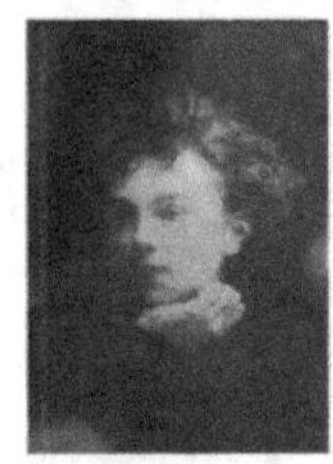
Thomas Hardy: Selected Poems
Percy Bysshe Shelley: Poems
John Keats: Selected Poems
Joh n Keats: Poems of 1820
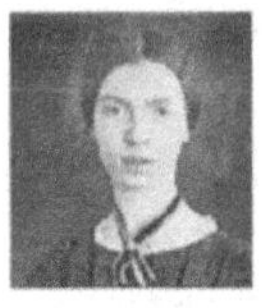
D.H. Lawrence: Selected Poems
Edmund Spenser: Poems
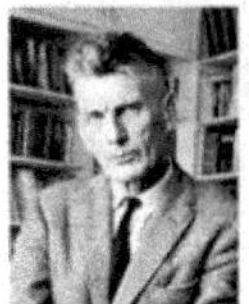
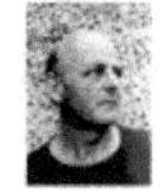
Edmund Spenser: Amoretti
John Donne: Poems
Henry Vaughan: Poems
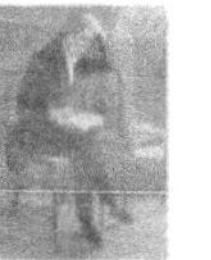
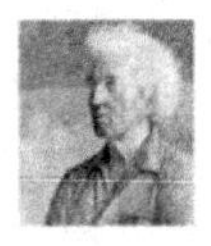
Sir Thomas Wyatt: Poems
Robert Herrick: Selected Poems
Rilke: Space, Essence and Angels in the Poetry of Rainer Maria Rilke
Rainer Maria Rilke: Selected Poems
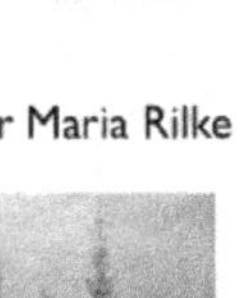
Friedrich Hölderlin: Selected Poems
Arseny Tarkovsky: Selected Poems
Arthur Rimbaud: Selected Poems
Arthur Rimbaud: A Season in Hell
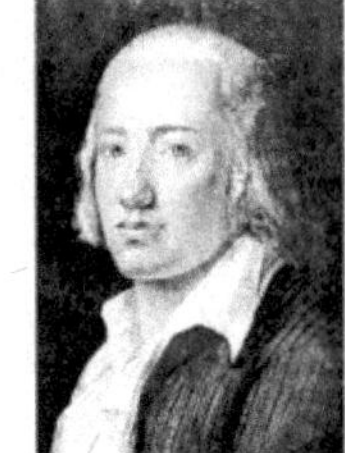
Arthur Rimbaud and the Magic of Poetry
Novalis: Hymns To the Night
German Romantic Poetry
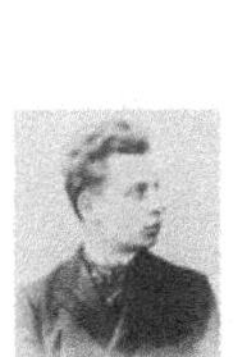
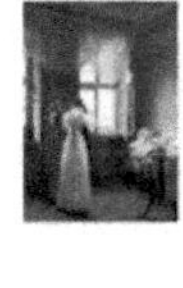
Paul Verlaine: Selected Poems
Elizaethan Sonnet Cycles
D.J. Enright: By-Blows
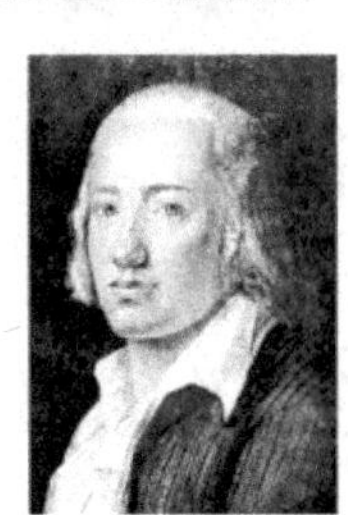
Jeremy Reed: Brigitte's Blue Heart
Jeremy Reed: Claudia Schiffer's Red Shoes
Gorgeous Little Orpheus
Radiance: New Poems
Crescent Moon Book of Nature Poetry
Crescent Moon Book of Love Poetry
Crescent Moon Book of Mystical Poetry
Crescent Moon Book of Elizabethan Love Poetry
Crescent Moon Book of Metaphysical Poetry
Crescent Moon Book of Romantic Poetry
Pagan America: New American Poetry

MEDIA, CINEMA, FEMINISM and CULTURAL STUDIES

J.R.R. Tolkien: The Books, The Films, The Whole Cultural Phenomenon
J.R.R. Tolkien: Pocket Guide
The *Lord of the Rings* Movies: Pocket Guide
The Cinema of Hayao Miyazaki
Hayao Miyazaki: *Princess Mononoke*: Pocket Movie Guide
Hayao Miyazaki: *Spirited Away*: Pocket Movie Guide
Tim Burton : Hallowe'en For Hollywood
Ken Russell
Ken Russell: *Tommy*: Pocket Movie Guide
The Ghost Dance: The Origins of Religion
The Peyote Cult
Cixous, Irigaray, Kristeva: The *Jouissance* of French Feminism
Julia Kristeva: Art, Love, Melancholy, Philosophy, Semiotics and Psychoanalysis
Luce Irigaray: Lips, Kissing, and the Politics of Sexual Difference
Hélene Cixous I Love You: The *Jouissance* of Writing
Andrea Dworkin
'Cosmo Woman': The World of Women's Magazines
Women in Pop Music
HomeGround: The Kate Bush Anthology
Discovering the Goddess (Geoffrey Ashe)
The Poetry of Cinema
The Sacred Cinema of Andrei Tarkovsky
Andrei Tarkovsky: Pocket Guide
Andrei Tarkovsky: *Mirror*: Pocket Movie Guide
Andrei Tarkovsky: *The Sacrifice*: Pocket Movie Guide
Walerian Borowczyk: Cinema of Erotic Dreams
Jean-Luc Godard: The Passion of Cinema
Jean-Luc Godard: *Hail Mary*: Pocket Movie Guide
Jean-Luc Godard: *Contempt*: Pocket Movie Guide
Jean-Luc Godard: *Pierrot le Fou*: Pocket Movie Guide
John Hughes and Eighties Cinema
Ferris Bueller's Day Off: Pocket Movie Guide
Jean-Luc Godard: Pocket Guide
The Cinema of Richard Linklater
Liv Tyler: Star In Ascendance
Blade Runner and the Films of Philip K. Dick
Paul Bowles and Bernardo Bertolucci
Media Hell: Radio, TV and the Press
An Open Letter to the BBC
Detonation Britain: Nuclear War in the UK
Feminism and Shakespeare
Wild Zones: Pornography, Art and Feminism
Sex in Art: Pornography and Pleasure in Painting and Sculpture
Sexing Hardy: Thomas Hardy and Feminism

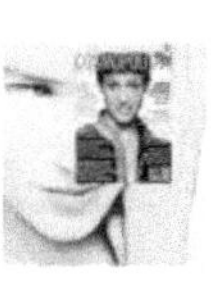
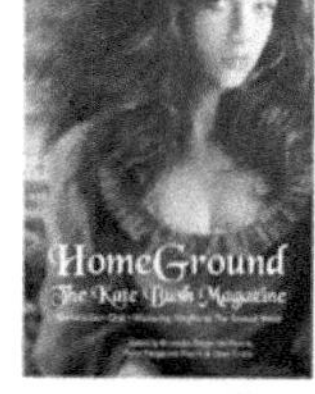
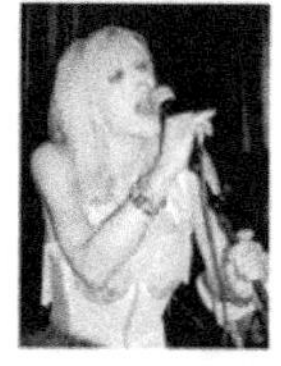
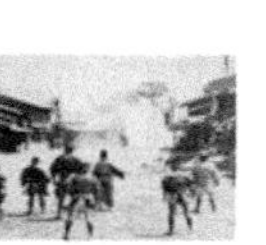
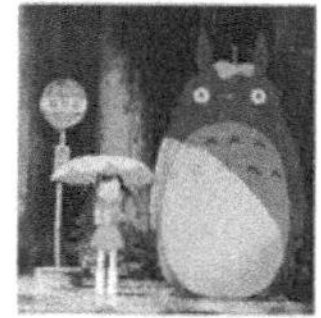
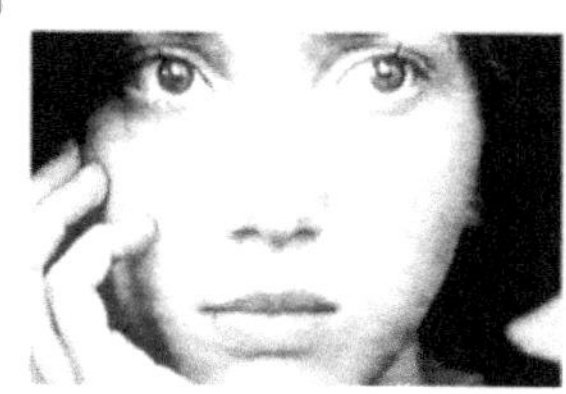

The Light Eternal is a model monograph, an exemplary job. The subject matter of the book is beautifully
organised and dead on beam. (Lawrence Durrell)
It is amazing for me to see my work treated with such passion and respect. (Andrea Dworkin)

CRESCENT MOON PUBLISHING
P.O. Box 1312, Maidstone, Kent, ME14 5XU, Great Britain. www.crmoon.com

cresmopub@yahoo.co.uk   www.crescentmoon.org.uk

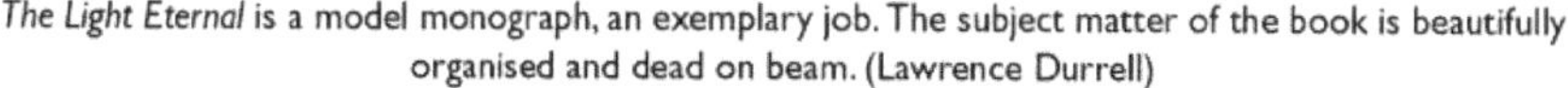

9 781861 716217